Myers'

THE NORTH EAST

Also by Alan Myers

Brodsky *Democracy* (Granta)
Brodsky *Marble* (Penguin)
Dostoevsky *The Idiot* (OUP)
Dostoevsky *A Gentle Creature and other stories* (OUP)
Pushkin *Prose Tales* (OUP)
Topol *Red Gas* (Macdonald)

MYERS'
LITERARY
GUIDE

The North East

ALAN MYERS

1995
Mid Northumberland Arts Group
Carcanet Press

First published in Great Britain in 1995
by the Mid Northumberland Arts Group
Wansbeck Square, Ashington
Northumberland and
Carcanet Press Limited
402–406 Corn Exchange Buildings,
Manchester M4 3BY

A CIP catalogue record for this book
is available from the British Library

ISBN [MidNAG] 0 904790 86 X
ISBN [Carcanet] 1 85754 199 5

Carcanet Press acknowledges financial assistance
from the Arts Council of England

Set in 9/10pt Plantin
by Servis Filmsetting Ltd, Manchester
Printed and bound by SRP Ltd, Exeter

Contents

Acknowledgements

The publishers and author would like to thank the following: Oxford University Press for permission to quote from *The Adventures of Mr Verdant Green*, 1982, by 'Cuthbert Bede', and *Collected Poems*, 1978, by Basil Bunting; Faber and Faber Limited for *Collected Poems* ('New Year Letter') by W. H. Auden, and *Collected Poems* ('Hymn to the Sun') by Michael Roberts; Virago Press Limited for *A Note in Music* by Rosamond Lehmann; Victor Gollancz Limited for *The Stars Look Down* by A. J. Cronin; HarperCollins Publishers Limited for *The Selected Letters of E. M. Forster*, vol. 1, 1985, edited by Mary Lago and P. N. Furbank.

The cover illustration is 'Iron and Coal', by William Bell Scott, from the Central Hall, Wallington, Northumberland – a property of the National Trust.

Support for the publication has been kindly provided by Northern Electric plc, together with the Arts Council of England and Northern Arts.

Publishers' Note

The North East includes the counties of Northumberland, Tyne and Wear, Durham, and Cleveland.

Introduction

It is a matter for pride that one area of the country should be able to claim both the first known writer of English prose and the first English Christian poet. That eminent literary figures having important links with the same area should also include Wordsworth and Coleridge, Forster and Conrad, Auden and Larkin, no fewer than nine authors of classic children's stories, six pioneer feminists, a famous French revolutionary, Portugal's greatest novelist, a Pope and a Roman Emperor, not to mention two relatives of the Queen Mother, is one reason for gathering this rich profusion into book form.

Another purpose in commemorating the mighty dead in this fashion has been to adjust a cultural imbalance. Much of the information contained in the present volume is extremely hard to come by in the standard reference and biographical sources. Harriet Martineau's five productive years in Tynemouth, Algernon Swinburne's fervent Northumberland patriotism, and W. H. Auden's lifelong obsession with the North Pennines, to take examples at random, are usually omitted, or receive no more than a passing mention. Even librarians are often unaware that writers of national significance have local associations. As a consequence, an enormous amount of negative research has been necessary, culminating, more often than not, in recourse to original diaries, letters or complete works. In some cases, surviving relatives could be contacted: their help was uniquely valuable and is here gratefully acknowledged.

Of course, no conspiracy theory need be invoked to explain this neglectful treatment of the North East. It is simply that reference books feed off one another: once the literary map of the region had been written off as uneventful, compared, say, with the Thames Valley, later compilers naturally followed suit. Until now, no one has been obsessively patriotic enough to expend time and energy in disputing the accuracy of the accepted picture, especially when it might involve a good deal of original research.

After the golden age of Northumbria had ended in the early ninth century with the coming of the Vikings, the war-zone status, formidable terrain and sparse population of the region in the Middle Ages were reasons enough for believing the North East an unlikely habitation for the muses. Language served as another isolating factor. Northumbrian, up to the eleventh century, was one of the four main English dialects. It proved resistant to change, however, and over time became marginalised by East Midland speech, which, as the language of the court and the universities, was eventually accepted as standard. By the fourteenth century, though it was still normal for writers to use their regional dialect, Geoffrey Chaucer could give the two likeable students in his *Reeve's Tale* a northern accent and idiom, almost certainly as a comic device.

Hadrian's Wall had remained a permanent and tangible symbol of a frontier with the wilderness, and Northumberland as a grim embattled wasteland is a recurring picture. The voluminous Italian writer, Aeneas Silvius Piccolomini (later Pope Pius II) visited the region in 1435, while travelling to Scotland disguised as a merchant. He clearly regarded Newcastle as the last outpost of civilisation. Long after the Anglo-Scottish conflict had subsided, Lady Elizabeth Montagu pretended to think that the town lay beyond the Arctic Circle, while Jane Austen, in *Pride and Prejudice*, packs off her erring lovers to Newcastle, the furthest English town she could think of. Curiously, the idea of remoteness never seems to attach to Edinburgh, proving that every country, including Scotland, has a north and south.

This perceived isolation from the settled and cultivated Home Counties, reinforced by a persistent attachment to losing historical causes, has often been transferred, by way of the pathetic fallacy, to the weather. Though the populated parts of the North East are among the driest in Britain, and January temperatures are higher than, say, inland East Anglia or the Thames Valley, the weather is usually spoken of by natives and outsiders alike as uniquely atrocious. Writers who knew the area only in winter – Lord Byron, Ivor Gurney and J. B. Priestley, for example – take a gloomy view. Those who knew it all the year round are those who feel most passionately about it: Penelope Gilliatt, Swinburne, John Wesley. Even the melancholy Larkin felt his mood lift during his Haydon Bridge holidays. On such banal considerations may the literary image of a whole region occasionally turn.

The development of the coal industry was a cause for pride and fascination to the Elizabethans, who likened the rich North East coalfield to the Spanish mines in Peru, and dubbed it the 'Black Indies'. Literature, however, was still considered to be the product of a more leisured and refined society. The Border ballads, admittedly, were admired by such as Ben Jonson and Sir Philip Sidney, but the latter's celebrated remark about being thrilled by 'the old song of Percy and Douglas' is prefaced by the words: 'Certainly I must confess my own barbarousness', a telling phrase. In the seventeenth century, Thomas Burrough, the Quaker, prefaces his laudatory remarks with: 'O thou North of England, who art counted as desolate and barren, and reckoned the least of the nations . . .' Doctor Johnson's jeering remark that Scots went to Newcastle to be 'polished by colliers' reflects something of the same sentiment.

The Romantic movement made the Lakes a desirable literary residence and tourist destination, but the Eden valley was a sharp boundary of sensibility. No one sought visions of God in nature among the lead mines. Though the nineteenth century was one period when the capital lost its traditional dominance, the growth of manufacturing in the great cities of the north and midlands found little but disparagement in London literary circles. Victorian Manchester has been called a combination of modern Tokyo and Hong Kong, with its own banks, economists, charismatic members of parliament, even its own influential national newspaper. Dickens saw it as 'Coketown', aesthetically offensive and spiritually null.

Rather than describe the workshop of the world, he preferred to write about the London commercial and professional bourgeoisie: his poor are not the industrial poor. Trollope might treat of railway speculators, but not railway builders. Though the world of the future was, to a great extent, being forged elsewhere, the tendency among London writers was to regard the capital or the country as the only acceptable places of residence, a preference which dictated their subject matter. The north remained, in the literary sense, isolated, as the continent was by fog in the Channel.

Talented writers came perforce to the capital to seek recognition. They became metropolitan personalities and appeared in one another's diaries and letters; they wrote for Dickens or Ford Madox Ford; they encountered Henry James in Pall Mall; they lived together in Chelsea or Bloomsbury. Biographical material and reminiscence in this crowded milieu is plentiful, and completely overshadows any provincial connection. This is deemed of little significance, and usually consists in a vague reference to 'the north of England' when evaluating a writer's achievement.

For those who stayed outside the London literary ambit, matters are even worse. A richly comic writer like Surtees, for example, can have the adjective 'faceless' applied to him, simply because metropolitan material is not available. Moreover, the perennial cultural trap, 'unfamiliar equals inferior', means that adjectives like 'little-known' or 'unsung' begin to sound like accusations, rather than admissions of critical laziness or metropolitan complacency.

The industrial depression of the 1930s saw the North East, no longer the home of awesome, though repellent, Promethean industry, become the safari destination of literary figures randy for reportage. Aldous Huxley's essay title 'Abroad in England' might stand for all such assignments – and speaks directly and exclusively to a metropolitan audience. The tradition is still flourishing today, with newspapers, especially their weekend magazines, giving grimly downbeat accounts, accompanied by dark photographs, of their freelance reporter's brief sojourn in 'this region of chronic decline'.

A resistance movement is overdue. One may smile at the London obsession with putting up a plaque where James Joyce once paused for thought, or Zola stayed the night, but in an exhibitionist age like ours, modesty all too often invites neglect and oblivion. For a city like Newcastle, with a thousand years of history, to have only a single literary plaque (to Jack Common in Heaton), is surely carrying the Geordie detestation of 'the porrige of outside show' too far. The centenary commemoration of Elinor Brent-Dyer in South Shields received national coverage, and perhaps should set an example. Robert Westall has also recently received his due with a plaque and trail in North Tyneside only a year after his death.

To make exaggerated claims for the area as a nest of singing birds, or to over-promote writers of purely local significance, would, of course, be provincial. Masochistic/Self-hating silence about the literary associations of the area, on the other hand, allows all sorts of casual behaviour to creep in unchallenged. Ray Monk, in his fine biography, has Wittgenstein living in a district of Newcastle called Brandling Park (it's a street); Lady Lytton's dramatic account of her imprisonment and hunger strike in Newcastle is quietly transferred to London in a TV suffragette series; Andrew Motion's splendid life of Larkin meticulously locates every restaurant, but puts two Weardale villages in Northumberland. No one comments; it is not very serious. But would it happen in the Home Counties?

Such sins of commission, however, are far outweighed by those of omission mentioned earlier. This book aims to prove the situation unjust, and further contends that neither shrill declamation nor pained silence is appropriate where the literary history of the North East is concerned. Instead, it seeks to provide a solid – and enjoyable – justification for civilised self-assertion.

Anyone embarking on a task like this must turn first of all to the older volumes of the *Dictionary of National Biography*, and the monumental eleventh edition of *Britannica* (1910). R. J. Charleton's *Newcastle Town* (1885) is both diverting and instructive. For details of women writers, the *Feminist Companion to Literature in English* (Batsford) has been invaluable. Architectural comments are based on the uniquely magnificent *Buildings of England* series (Penguin) edited for so long by Sir Nikolaus Pevsner.

Particular thanks are also due to Miss Margaret Norwell at the library of the Lit and Phil in Newcastle, as well as the local studies librarians in South Shields and Sunderland. It is hoped that the multitude of other people who have responded cheerfully to persistent and tedious questioning will feel recompensed by seeing their contribution within.

To lay claim to extensive original research is to admit corresponding responsibility for errors of fact and interpretation. It also goes without saying that the author will be only too pleased to accept any assistance in shedding further light in an area that has remained dark too long.

Myers' Literary Guide

THE NORTH EAST

Mark Akenside (1721–1770)

The Newcastle poet-physician was born at 33 Butcher Bank (now Akenside Hill). The son of a butcher, he was rendered lame by an accident with his father's cleaver. Trained in Edinburgh and abroad, Akenside eventually rose to be physician to the queen at the accession of George III in 1763.

Akenside was very touchy about his humble origins; possibly as a result, he gained the reputation of behaving roughly to the poor, especially to women. He was not an easy man to like, despite being ready to praise other poets; he had annoyed the testy Scottish novelist Tobias Smollett by disparaging Scotland, and was consequently satirised as the conceited and pedantic doctor in *Peregrine Pickle*.

In Newcastle, Akenside wrote a number of minor poems for *The Gentleman's Magazine*, including 'A Hymn to Science', but it was while visiting relations at Morpeth that he conceived the plan for *The Pleasures of Imagination* (1744), his most celebrated work. It is a long, erudite and complex poem, which takes on the difficult task of rendering a philosophical treatise in verse. Dr Johnson was not an admirer: 'The words are multiplied till the sense is hardly perceived.' There are occasional striking passages, but it has to be admitted that there is much leaden verse, stuffed with classical allusions. Recalling his youth by the 'dales of Tyne' and the Wansbeck however, Akenside finds more immediacy:

> . . . O ye Northumbrian shades! which overlook
> The rocky pavement and the mossy falls
> Of solitary Wensbeck's limpid stream,
> How gladly I recall your well-known seats,
> Beloved of old

Anonymous

At first known as miracle plays, dramatisations of biblical stories were popular in the Middle Ages from the thirteenth to the sixteenth centuries. The Passion Play at Oberammergau is a modern survival. In 1311, the Feast of Corpus Christi was established as a holy day and provided a focus for the plays, which were performed all over England, often on pageant wagons, before a festive audience. The trade guilds were usually entrusted with production, each working on individual episodes. Hence they became known as 'mystery' plays, from the word *mestier/metier*, meaning a trade. A few complete cycles of mystery plays in verse have survived, notably from Chester, York and Wakefield. Though religious in subject matter, the plays were realistic in performance and designed to entertain.

Newcastle had a cycle of 12 plays, performed, according to the Rev. Henry Bourne, the Newcastle historian, on Corpus Christi Day. It was a colourful occasion with banners, music, church bells, and marches to places of performance like the Spital and the Sandhill. The Shipwrights' enactment of Noah's Ark is the only one to have survived: it included an angel, Noah's wife and the Devil. The earliest performance of the plays in Newcastle is said to be 1426, but this seems rather late. Declining in 1578, they were suppressed in the 1600s, as a result of Reformation opposition to the idolatry and pageantry associated with Catholicism.

The apprentice boys of Newcastle, whose saucy complaint of having too much salmon to eat is well known, also kept falling foul of the Puritan tendency. An Act of the Merchant Adventurers of 1554 thunders against their gay dress and 'tippling and dancing . . . what use of gitternes [guitars] by night!' In 1603, the youths are again enjoined 'not to dance or use music in the streets at night': nor are they to deck themselves in velvet and lace – or to wear their 'locks at their ears like ruffians'. All to no avail; in 1649, Newcastle's Puritan elders were still railing against ribbons and lace, gold and silver thread, and coloured shoes of Spanish leather. Nine recalcitrant youths received the pudding-basin treatment for their hair.

Arthurian Legend

The existence of an historical King Arthur figure, as opposed to the glorious fiction of Camelot, is very problematic. He was a folk hero as early as the ninth century, but the (unreliable) historical sources are vague and confusing. Northern battle sites are certainly mentioned, including High Rochester in Northumberland (the Roman fort Bremenium), and one chronicle refers to the fight at Camlann, supposedly in AD 537, 'where Arthur and Medraut were killed'.

Opinion concerning the location of Camlann favours Camboglanna, close to the Roman fort at Birdoswald on the Wall. The Camlann battle became a byword for a tragic, irretrievable disaster, as Michael Wood puts it in his book *In Search of the Dark Ages*. We also know that 'Medraut' became the traitor figure Mordred in the later Arthurian legends. Could a struggle between obscure chieftains on the edge of Northumberland have given rise to one of the greatest figures in world literature?

Sir Thomas Malory (d. 1471), the author of *Le Morte D'Arthur* places the Joyous Gard, Sir Lancelot's castle, somewhere in the north, either at Alnwick or Bamburgh. When Queen Guinevere is sentenced to death at Carlisle, Lancelot rescues her and takes her off to Joyous Gard, where he is soon besieged by King Arthur's knights. Though well-known to us through Malory's noble prose and Tennyson's memorable verse, Lancelot's personality is rather dull compared to Gawain, Perceval and Tristan (Tristram). Merlin's master, the hermit Blaise, dwelt in the forests of Northumberland, according to Malory, who is followed by Tennyson.

Malory says that Tristram kept Isoud at Joyous Gard for three years, and Algernon Swinburne in his *Tristram and Iseult*, describes Bamburgh Castle, '. . . this noblest hold of all the north,' in thrilling verse:

> They saw the strength and help of Joyous Gard.
> Within the full deep glorious tower that stands
> Between the wild sea and the broad wild lands

The story of Balyn and Balan, two knights who slay one another after a series of linked adventures, is recounted by Malory in the second book of *Morte D'Arthur*. Swinburne, in 1896, based his *Tale of Balen* on this, coupling with it an ecstatic celebration of Northumberland and his own youth as a reckless horseman riding 'the northland border'.

The Hexham-born poet Wilfrid Gibson, incidentally, places

Joyous Gard at Dunstanburgh in an effectively atmospheric poem.

Lord Tennyson's aunt married Matthew Russell of the wealthy Sunderland family. From 1818 onwards, Russell spent vast sums in giving the old Neville stronghold at Brancepeth the mediaeval (or Arthurian) look it has today. The church at Brancepeth was not altered, however, and contains, as well as Bishop Cosin's sumptuous woodwork, the tomb of Ralph Neville, 'the peacock of the North', slain by the Douglas in 1319.

Tennyson was invited to Brancepeth Castle for his honeymoon in 1850, but in the end went to the Lake District, where he had spent time in his youth. It had then supplied the backdrop for his celebrated poem *Morte d'Arthur*; now it produced the Arthurian *Idylls of the King*, which includes the phrase 'crag-carved above the streaming Gelt'. The Gelt is a tributary of the Eden, and rises high in the North Pennines on the Northumberland border.

Whether Tennyson ever visited Brancepeth is unclear, but according to Henry Thorold in the *Shell Guide*, he composed the following lines (source untraced):

> Far and near
> From every side come noisy swarms
> Of peasants in their homely gear,
> And mixed with these to Brancepeth came
> Grave gentry of estate and name,
> And captains known for worth in arms.

Mary Astell (1666–1731)

Mary Astell, one of the pioneering feminists of England, was born in the Quayside area of Newcastle and educated by her uncle in Latin, French, logic, mathematics and natural philosophy. She was writing religious poetry of high quality by 1687, and had settled alone in Chelsea.

In 1694, she published *A Serious Proposal to the Ladies* which put forward the idea of a kind of monastery or university for unmarried women. It would also act as a haven for women evading a mercenary marriage, or the fate of being a derided spinster. The question is posed: 'What poor woman is ever taught that she should have a higher design than to get her a husband?'

Mary Astell supported the Church of England and the establishment in general, and is therefore regarded as belonging to the right wing of feminist thought. She has been called 'incalculably influential' and Daniel Defoe was not above borrowing her ideas. A formidable opponent in written argument, she believed in the equal intellectual and spiritual capacities of the two sexes. In 1700 her tract *Some Reflections upon Marriage* supported the idea of a companionate marriage; the preface to the 1706 edition asks: 'If all men are born free, how is it that all women are born slaves?'

Wystan Hugh Auden (1907–1973)

Though the great poet had little mechanical aptitude, he acquired in childhood a lifelong fascination with underground spaces and mining machinery. His family bought a holiday cottage near Keswick in the early 1920s, and Auden stayed there frequently until his depar-

3

ture for America in 1939. It was Alston Moor, however, and the adjoining region of Durham and Northumberland, with its poignant remains of a great lead mining industry, which Auden came to love more than any other locality.

Among the poet's juvenilia we find a poem of the early 1920s entitled 'The North' which joyously celebrates the high fell country. 'Alston Moor' and 'Allendale' also date from 1924, as does the poem entitled 'Rookhope (Weardale, Summer 1922)'. What Auden indicated as the seminal moment in his creative life seems to have occurred when he dropped a stone down an abandoned mine shaft in Rookhope, probably in that summer of 1922. It is a recurring image in his verse. Auden describes the hard life of the lead miner (and alludes to the Border ballads) in his 'Lead's the Best' of 1926. His 'charade' *Paid on Both Sides* (1928) openly uses Pennine village names – Rookhope, and Garrigill for example. Indeed, the two houses in the play, Lintzgarth Mill (close to Rookhope), and Nattrass, still stand. London reviewers took these strange names to be inventions.

At Easter 1930, Auden and his friend Gabriel Carritt stayed at the Lord Crewe Arms in Blanchland after a walk along the Roman Wall. Carritt recalls Auden loudly calling for champagne in the public bar, before striding over to the 'honky-tonk' piano and launching into Brahms. Next day, the pair bathed in the freezing Derwent before setting off to inspect abandoned mine workings. Auden's poetry and plays at this period are studded with references to northern locations. *The Dog Beneath the Skin* (1935), for example, mentions Bellingham and Scot's Gap, together with a sonorous roll-call of Pennine fells. The village of Pressan Ambo in the drama is probably based on Blanchland.

On 25 November 1937, Auden and Benjamin Britten were present for the broadcast of their radio documentary *Hadrian's Wall*, from the studios in New Bridge Street in Newcastle. Britten's setting of perhaps the most celebrated section, 'Roman Wall Blues' has, alas, been lost. Auden introduced Britten to Janet Adam Smith and Michael Roberts, whom he had visited in Jesmond that September.

On Sunday, 17 December 1972, Auden was once more in Newcastle, reading in the University Theatre, Haymarket. He performed in carpet slippers, as was his wont in later years. The reading was organised by George Stephenson of the Mid Northumberland Arts Group (MidNAG), who recalls that the sound system left a lot to be desired! While in the city, Auden stayed at the Turk's Head in Grey Street. It is fitting that the last completed readings of his life (in Newcastle and Ilkley) should take place close to the landscapes he cherished. Perhaps the ringing lines from 'New Year Letter' (1940) can stand as testimony to what the northern hills meant to one of the great poets of our century:

> An English area comes to mind,
> I see the nature of my kind
> As a locality I love,
> Those limestome moors that stretch from BROUGH
> To HEXHAM and the ROMAN WALL.
> There is my symbol of us all.

4

. . . .
Always my boy of wish returns
To those peat-stained deserted burns
That feed the WEAR and TYNE and TEES . . .

Richard Aungerville (1287–1345)

Nearly all the powers the king had elsewhere belonged to the mediaeval Bishop of Durham. He had his own parliament (Durham sent
no representatives to London) and his own coinage; soldiers fought
under him, not the king; all mines belonged to him and he had the
power of capital punishment.

Some bishops were warriors (preferring the mace as weapon), like
the flamboyant Anthony Bek; others were builders, like Hugh
Pudsey – and Thomas Hatfield, who provided the prince bishops
with the highest throne in Christendom. *Domesday Book* (1086) had
not included the North East, and Bishop Pudsey's great survey,
known as the *Boldon Book* (1183), provides a vast store of information about the palatinate in the late twelfth century. It is a priceless
document and historians owe Pudsey a debt.

Richard Aungerville had taken part in the grim intrigues surrounding the deposition and gruesome murder of Edward II. On the
accession of Edward III, whose tutor he had been, he achieved rapid
promotion. Edward appointed him Bishop of Durham in 1333
(against the wishes of the monks) and the enthronement in Durham
Cathedral was attended by the King and Queen of England, the King
of Scotland and many high dignitaries.

On an embassy in 1330 to the Pope in Avignon, Aungerville had
met the great Petrarch, who considered the Englishman 'not ignorant of literature'. Now Aungerville began to collect manuscripts from
far and wide: 'No dearness of price ought to hinder a man from the
buying of books if he has the money demanded for them, unless it be
to withstand the malice of the seller or to await a more favourable
opportunity of buying.' Indeed, presents of books could often secure
Aungerville's support in some matter. To him belongs, it seems, the
honour of founding the first lending library in England – at Durham
College in Oxford (now Trinity College), to which Durham students
were sent between c 1326 and 1544. He wrote about his passion for
books and his plans for a library in his Latin *Philobiblon* (1345), the
year he died at Auckland Castle.

Another scholar and statesman to have occupied the bishopric
(1530–59) was Cuthbert Tunstall, the friend of Erasmus and Thomas
More. Tunstall was also the great-uncle and protector of the saintly
Bernard Gilpin (1517–83), the 'Apostle of the North'. It was in
Tunstall's time that the idea for a college at Durham was first
mooted, a project revived in 1604. A proposal for a university in
Durham was discussed between 1649 and 1659, but was repelled by
Oxford and Cambridge.

The suppression of the monasteries, and northern opposition to
the Tudor monarchs' religious policy in Tunstall's time ended the
great power of the bishops of Durham. Nevertheless, the tradition of
scholarship continued and it remains the case that, after a thousand
years, when the Bishop of Durham speaks, he is heard.

Charles Avison (1710–1770)

Charles Avison, the celebrated Newcastle organist and composer, is buried in St Andrew's churchyard. In 1752, he published his important *Essay on Musical Expression*, the first English treatise on musical criticism. Despite offers from London, York and Dublin, Avison preferred to remain in Newcastle.

Robert Browning makes him the subject of one of the best of his *Parleyings with Certain People*, referring to him as 'Thou, whilom of Newcastle organist!' and saying how much he enjoyed his 'Grand March':

> Hear Avison! He tenders evidence
> That music in his day as much absorbed
> Heart and soul then as Wagner's music now . . .

Barnabe Barnes (1569–1609)

A younger son of Richard Barnes, Bishop of Durham, Barnes fought in the Earl of Essex's forces in France in 1591. The collection of love poems on which his fame rests was printed two years later; entitled *Parthenophil and Parthenope*, only one copy is known to exist. Barnes was attacked by the celebrated Thomas Nashe, who accused him, among other things, of cowardice in the face of the enemy and making himself a laughing-stock by wearing 'Babilonian britches'. Barnes is also mentioned by Thomas Campion under the name of Barnzy, in 1602; he had previously written bluntly of Barnes as a braggart and a coward.

Barnes' second book, *A Divine Centurie of Spirituall Sonnets* appeared in 1595. Three years later he attempted to murder the recorder of Berwick using poisoned claret, but seems to have escaped punishment by fleeing to Durham.

His last work was a tragedy called *The Divil's Charter* (1607). This has been decried as unpleasant, even nauseous reading for the most part, but not without some powerful passages. Shakespeare is said to have borrowed some business from it. It includes the murder of Lucrezia Borgia with poisoned face-wash. Barnes was an accomplished minor Elizabethan poet, with the rich, euphuistic writing then fashionable. According to the registers of St Mary-le-Bow in Durham, Barnes was buried there in December 1609.

Bede (AD 673–735)

Bede was probably born in Monkton and went to school at Wearmouth monastery. Founded in AD 674 by Benedict Biscop, this was a stone edifice with glazed windows: indeed Biscop is credited with introducing both techniques to Saxon England. Biscop also brought back a store of books from Rome to furnish the monasteries at Wearmouth and Jarrow; on his death he left directions for the preservation of his library. Biscop is regarded as one of the originators of the artistic and literary development of Northumbria in the next century and is celebrated by Bede in his important work *Lives of the Abbots* (AD 716–720).

In St Paul's church, Jarrow, may be seen the oldest church dedicatory inscription in the country, dated 23 April AD 685. Bede transferred to Jarrow around this date and afterwards rarely left its confines. He became a priest at the age of 30 and taught Latin and Greek to the monks, but his scholarly interests were very wide and included medicine and astronomy. His earliest work was probably *De Orthographia*, a treatise on spelling. Bede wrote some forty religious works at Jarrow, including, in AD 731, his celebrated *Historia Ecclesiastica Gentis Anglorum*, sometimes translated as the *History of the English Church and People*. This remains the most valuable single source for the early history of Britain, and has earned him the title 'The Father of English History'. It includes the wonderful simile, which likens human life to the flight of a sparrow through a lighted hall, from darkness into darkness. The work traces the development of the Christian church from the fragmented groups which existed after the withdrawal of Roman troops, through to the consolidation of the faith under the influence of such figures as the Saints Patrick, David, Aidan and Columba.

The monastery on Lindisfarne or Holy Island was founded by Saint Aidan in AD 635. The *Lindisfarne Gospels*, written in the Latin Vulgate text in AD 698, probably in honour of the canonisation of Saint Cuthbert, are surpassed in grandeur only by the Irish *Book of Kells*. They are one of the greatest treasures of the British Museum. An Anglo-Saxon gloss was added in the late tenth century in the Northumbrian dialect, the translation being by Aldred of Chester-le-Street. Bede, in his moving *Life of Saint Cuthbert* tells of the holy man's life on Lindisfarne and in his cell on Inner Farne, where he died in AD 687. Cuthbert, the shepherd who tended his flocks near Doddington in Glendale, was the most popular saint in England from AD 687 to the canonisation of Thomas Becket in 1175 – indeed the mighty cathedral at Durham, the grandest Romanesque building in Europe, exists, in effect, as the shrine of this simple man.

As a historian, Bede was painstaking in the verification of fact and Lord Dacre calls him: 'The greatest scholar of his time, the greatest historian of the whole Middle Ages.' In addition, Bede's style is lively and gives many insights into the daily life of his time. Bede is the first known writer of English prose, and probably the best-known writer in western Europe throughout the early Middle Ages. His eminence is confirmed by the fact that he is the only Englishman to be named in Dante's *Paradiso* (c 1314).

A letter of his pupil Cuthbert gives a famous account of Bede's death in AD 735. Bede was made a saint in 1899, though he had been called 'Venerabilis' as early as the ninth century. His tomb may be seen in the Galilee Chapel in Durham Cathedral.

Cuthbert Bede (1827–1889)

Edward Bradley's popular book *The Adventures of Mr Verdant Green*, originally published in three parts in the 1850s, is the best-known of his 26 works, and chronicles the life of a freshman at Oxford. Bradley himself had attended University College in Durham, graduating BA in 1848, but then went to Oxford to spend a year or so studying to enter the church. Bradley's pseudonym derives of course from the two saints buried in Durham Cathedral; he also named his first son Cuthbert. No fewer than nine chapters in Part III of the book are devoted to Verdant Green's visit to north Northumberland. On the way he passes through Darlington, where the porters proclaim the stations, 'Faweyill' and 'Fensoosen' and the alarming 'Change here for Doom!' After mentioning Durham Cathedral and Lord Durham's monument on Penshaw hill, Verdant Green and his party then pass:

> . . . with a scream and a rattle, over the wonderful High Level (then barely completed), looking down with a sort of self-satisfied shudder upon the bridge, and the Tyne, and the fleet of colliers, and the busy quays, and the quaint timber-built houses with their overlapping storeys, and picturesque black and white gables.

The location of 'Honeywood Hall', where Verdant's Northumberland adventures take place, is a matter of conjecture. It is certainly north of Alnwick, and The Cheviot lies behind it. The guests visit Warkworth, Alnwick, Ros Castle and Chillingham Castle to see the wild cattle. There is also a trip to Bamburgh and the Longstone light to talk to Grace Darling's father. Verdant himself eventually gets married in the ruinous 'Lasthope Church' whose description would fit Ingram church in the valley of the Breamish.

Bradley clearly knew the area well and gives an attractive picture of the wild landscape and the pleasures of riding, al fresco meals and neighbourly contact, the warmer for being more difficult than in crowded midland counties. Much amusement is had with local dialect and customs, but it is not condescending and the laugh is usually on Verdant Green.

Gertrude Bell (1868–1926)
In Washington Hall, a plaque records:

Gertrude Bell:
> Scholar, Historian, Archaeologist, Explorer, Poet, Mountaineer, Gardener, Distinguished servant of the State: Born here, 14 July 1868, died Baghdad, 12 July 1926.

Gertrude Bell, one of the most remarkable women of modern times, was the daughter of Hugh Lowthian Bell, ironmaster and colliery owner. The Bell house is now the Red Barnes (sic) Hotel, 31 Kirkleatham Street in Coatham, which adjoins Redcar. Inside the foyer, there are photographs of Gertrude and the family houses at Washington Hall and Rounton. Outside, there is a plaque com-memorating Gertrude, who lived here from the age of two. Her mother died a year later and it was her step-mother, Lady Frances (Olliffe) Bell who was to edit Gertrude's famous *Letters* (never out of print since 1927). Lady Bell was an author and playwright herself and her researches among the women of Teesside led to her classic study *At the Works* (1907).

It was at Red Barns that Gertrude's first childish letters were written, devoting much space to the Persian cat Mopsa. Gertrude always spelled certain words wrongly all her life – 'siezed', and 'excer-cised' among them! She was very happy at Redcar among her pets and flowers, riding her pony and outdoing her brother Maurice at climbing over the greenhouse. Later on, she took great pleasure in socialising in London and at Red Barns, her home till 1905.

Gertrude Bell achieved a First in Modern History at Oxford, an unprecedented feat for a woman. She then spent many years mountaineering and travelling in the desert lands of the Middle East, usually only with a guide and camel-train (though not without expensive clothes and crockery). 'By Allah!' an Arab is supposed to have said. 'What must their men be like?' She also made her name as a writer with *The Desert and the Sown* (1907) and other works, including a fine translation of the Persian poet Hafiz.

During and after World War I, she worked for the British government in the Middle East and helped to further Lawrence of Arabia's aims. She may thus be regarded as one of the founders of Iraq. Lawrence thought her 'a wonderful person'; she used to address him as 'Beloved Boy'. She is buried in Baghdad, where the great museum she founded is a fitting monument.

Gertrude Bell's life and accomplishments made her a celebrity wherever she went and the fact that she excelled at many things supposed to be the prerogative of men makes her a pioneer in opening the way for women of later generations. Like her father, however, she was not in favour of the Suffragettes. In fact in 1908, she became a founder member of the Woman's Anti-Suffrage League. This may be one reason why such a remarkable woman does not receive her full due today. She is, however, included in *The Virago Book of Women Travellers* (1994). Her papers are preserved at the University of Newcastle.

Sir Walter Besant (1836–1901)

Of all his many works, Sir Walter's own favourite was *Dorothy Forster* (1884), about the Northumberland heroine who rescued her brother 'General' Tom Forster from Newgate jail in London after the 1715 Jacobite rebellion, and enabled him to escape to France. Dorothy, disguised as a servant, rode pillion to London behind a village blacksmith and extricated her brother in a daring operation involving duplicate keys.

Blanchland was part of the Forster estates, forfeited after the rebellion, and Dorothy's ghost is said to haunt the Bamburgh Room in the Lord Crewe Arms. Though the novel takes some liberties with the events of Dorothy's life, the early sections are set in Blanchland. Dorothy's aunt and namesake married Nathaniel, Lord Crewe, Bishop of Durham (1674–1721), whose portrait by Kneller hangs in the hotel. It was the Crewe trustees who fashioned the idyllic village we see today.

Thomas Bewick (1753–1828)

The great wood engraver was born in Cherryburn, and the freshness of his work owes a great deal to the sights of his Tyne Valley childhood. A bust of Bewick marks the site behind the cathedral, where he and the Beilbys worked in Newcastle.

The success of his *General History of Quadrupeds* (1790) encouraged him to begin the *History of British Birds* and the later *Fables of Aesop*, all illustrated with delightful miniatures of birds, animals and human figures. Bewick illustrated many other publications and was admired by Wordsworth ('Oh that the genius of Bewick were mine'), Charles Kingsley, Ruskin and Thomas Carlyle. Charlotte Bronte wrote a poem about him, and the exciting book mentioned at the beginning of *Jane Eyre* was Bewick's *History of British Birds*.

John James Audubon, the great American painter and naturalist, visited the workshop in 1827, and writes in his journals that he found Bewick 'a perfect old Englishman' who worked in a soiled cotton night-cap. The American took tea with the family, while Bewick's son played the Northumbrian pipes. On a later visit, Audubon observed: 'His delicate and beautiful tools were all made by himself, and I may say with truth that his shop was the only artist's "shop" that I ever found perfectly clean and tidy.'

Bewick spent many late summer holidays at Tynemouth and began his famous *Memoir* there in November 1822, completing part by 10 December. It is a vivid record of his Cherryburn childhood and his life as a craftsman. It also includes a good deal of often sensible rumination on politics, education and religion, no doubt reflecting the talk at his favourite haunts in Newcastle, like the Fox and Lamb, and Swarley's Club in Groat Market, 'Newcastle's House of Lords'.

Bewick went to London but, despite favourable prospects, took an intense dislike to the place and returned home after nine months. He despised 'the porrige of outside show' and writes in a letter of 1776:

> Tho I might allway continue to meet with the greatest encouragement imajinable – yet wou'd I rather live in both poverty and insecurity in Ncastle. The Lord Mayor show – and all the numerous shows to be seen in London may give a momentary satisfaction – cannot afford me half the pleasure – which I allways felt in my excurtions . . . thro the pleasant woods to Eltringham . . .

Bewick's residence in Gateshead is commemorated on what is now the main post office in West Street, not far from the Gateshead Metro station. His last engraving shows a funeral procession winding slowly down from Cherryburn to the bridge across the Tyne. Bewick is buried in the churchyard at Ovingham. At Cherryburn, the farmhouse incorporates Bewick's birthplace and is now a museum devoted to the life and work of the 'Father of English Wood-Engraving'. Bewick's Swan was named in his honour shortly after his death.

James Boswell (1740–1795)

In the building now called White Knights in Spital Tongues, Newcastle, was a private asylum where Boswell used to visit his mentally unstable brother John. According to his journals, Boswell was there in May 1775 and again on 12 March 1776, when he reflected that it was better to have one's mind obscured than to be actively unhappy. John was able to recognise him and asked him for money. He then unexpectedly said: 'Take me with you.' Boswell was moved to tears, though he knew John was well looked after and was in no anguish of mind or body.

Samuel Johnson himself arrived in the city on Wednesday, 11 August 1773 on his way to join Boswell in Edinburgh for their celebrated tour of Scotland: he sent a note to Boswell from Newcastle, indicating that he would be arriving in Edinburgh on the Saturday. One of Johnson's frequent disparaging remarks about the Scots, incidentally, was that they went to Newcastle, 'to be polished by colliers'.

On his way through Northumberland it appears that Johnson, in pre-Romantic fashion, was 'repelled by the wide expanse of hopeless sterility'.

Mary Bowes, Countess of Strathmore (1749–1800)

The romantic shell of a great mansion on the banks of the Derwent, a beautiful Palladian chapel, and a 140 foot column to British Liberty (higher than Nelson's actual column) mark the site of Gibside. George Bowes, the coal magnate, was responsible for the park and its buildings, as well as the Great Walk stretching for over half a mile, along which he used to race his horses. In 1750, Lancelot 'Capability' Brown, born in Kirkharle, wrote to George Bowes, proposing himself as the architect of the monumental column: 'I should have a double pleasure in [building] it, your situation being my native country.'

George Bowes' daughter, Mary Eleanor, is the Queen Mother's great-great-grandmother. Mary wrote a play, *The Siege of Jerusalem*, but is better known for her extraordinary *Confessions*. Though she had five children by her handsome husband, she was not satisfied with one man. There was an affair with the brother of a local lord, followed by another with a certain George Grey. He is described in her *Confessions* as: 'a dishonest, lazy, amorous, greedy pussycat of a man'. She was already pregnant by him when her husband died aboard ship en route for Lisbon.

In 1776, the Countess married a romantic Irish desperado, Captain Andrew Stoney, who ill-treated her in public and private. The affair became the talk of London society. Stoney abducted Mary in Oxford Street after she instituted divorce proceedings, but was eventually apprehended at Streatlam Castle. His efforts to cling on to Mary's fortune failed and he died in prison. William Thackeray based his celebrated novel *The Luck of Barry Lyndon* partly on the scandal. The full story is told in Ralph Arnold's *The Unhappy Countess* (1957).

Augustus Hare later described Gibside as a beautiful place with 'exquisite woods feathering down to the Derwent'. There were two ghosts, he says, one being Lady Tyrconnel of the spirited Delaval family, who lived with John Bowes on rather too intimate terms. Her funeral almost bankrupted the estate; with painted face and decked in jewels and Brussels lace from head to toe, he had her lie in state in every town on the way to London and finally buried in Westminster Abbey.

Lilian Bowes-Lyon (1895–1949)

A cousin of the Queen Mother, Lilian Bowes-Lyon was born and grew up at Ridley Hall, near Riding Mill, where Augustus Hare stayed and described the haunting beauty of the grounds. Her observations of the country life she loved form the subject of her early poems, but after her move to the East End of London in 1942, her poetry is concentrated on the war. Her only novel *The Buried Stream* (1929) treats of the power of the unconscious.

Her verse appeared in many periodicals and her *Collected Poems* came out in 1948, when C. Day Lewis detected the influences of Emily Dickinson, Hopkins and Christina Rossetti. She suffered greatly from arthritis, and her last book of poems, *A Rough Walk Home* is as much about this as the war.

Her *Uncollected Poems*, not published until 1981, were written after she had lost both legs and the use of her hands. The poems include powerfully direct accounts of the pain she suffered. Her papers are in the William Plomer collection at the University of Durham.

John Braine (1922–1986)

According to the Penguin book-jacket, Joe Lampton, the thrusting hero of John Braine's best-seller *Room at the Top*, was raised in poverty and squalor in an ugly North Country town. The novelist's pungent prose, however, took shape, not in his native Bradford, but on slack afternoons in the peaceful purlieus of the library in Newbiggin by the Sea, where Braine worked between 1954 and 1956.

Elinor Brent-Dyer (1894–1969)

The famous *Chalet School* stories (1925–70), were written by Elinor Brent-Dyer, who was born at 52 Winchester Street in South Shields. She worked as a teacher in the town, and by 1933 had written 28 books in the attic bed-sitter at 5 Belgrave Terrace, including several notable Chalet School tales; in that year she accompanied her parents in their move to Hereford. Curiously enough, she was there when Catherine Cookson resided in Hereford during World War II, though there is no record of a meeting between South Shields' two most prolific and successful authors.

Unlike other girls' stories of that time, the Chalet School books remain hugely popular, regularly selling more than 150,000 a year. A centenary plaque has been erected in Westoe Village, South Shields, where the author herself attended school.

John Brown (1715–1766)

Brown, born in Rothbury, made his career in the church, but also wrote essays and poetry, as well as two plays in which David Garrick acted. His *Estimate of the Manners and Principles of the Times* (1757–58), castigating luxury during a time of war, was a popular success. It earned him the title of 'Estimate Brown'.

Brown became vicar of St Nicholas in Newcastle in January 1761. Invited two years later by Catherine the Great of Russia to be her adviser on education, he purchased a carriage and much else before the trip was cancelled at the last moment, supposedly because of a gout attack. It is thought that disappointment over this, coupled with a melancholic temperament, prompted his suicide in London.

John Brown (1810–1882)

The Scottish doctor and essayist was a frequent visitor at Wallington Hall. Keeping to his own admirable precept, that an author should publish nothing unless 'he has something to say and has done his best to say it aright', Brown published little. That little, however, includes his charming and humorous essays, and the celebrated dog story *Rab and his Friends* (1859), which achieved great popularity and became a volume in Dent's Everyman Library.

Elizabeth Barrett Browning (1806–1861)

Elizabeth Barrett was born at Coxhoe Hall (now demolished) in County Durham, where her father, Edward (Moulton) Barrett, had leased the house. She was christened in Kelloe church, where a plaque describes her as 'a great poetess, a noble woman, a devoted wife.' She spent the first three years of her life at Coxhoe.

Her mother Mary encouraged her daughter's talent, copying out her poems and tolerating, if not agreeing with, her feminist views.

Mary was the daughter of John Graham-Clarke of Kenton Lodge, and later Fenham Hall, in Newcastle, a merchant with extensive interests throughout the North East of England. The family also had a house at 92 Pilgrim Street.

While at school in England, after arriving from Jamaica, young Edward spent many jolly family holidays with the Graham-Clarkes, and eventually married Mary in St Nicholas, Church Road, South Gosforth (now close to the Metro station) in May 1805. The family lived in various parts of the country and did not become 'the Barretts of Wimpole Street' until 1835, seven years after Mary Barrett's death.

Margaret Forster's novel, *Lady's Maid*, shows the Brownings through the eyes of Elizabeth Wilson, a girl from Newcastle or nearby, who had worked in the Pilgrim Street house, and played a significant role in Elizabeth Barrett Browning's life both in England and Italy.

Elizabeth was an admirer of Harriet Martineau as a journalist and political economist, and also shared her detestation of slavery. As an invalid herself, she was thrilled to read of Harriet's recovery of her health through mesmerism – Harriet's maid mesmerised her twice a day – but feared to give control of herself to another person.

Basil Bunting (1900–1985)

Bunting, regarded as the first and principal British modernist poet, was born at 258 Denton Road, in what was then Scotswood-on-Tyne. The son of a cultivated doctor, he claimed descent from the Charltons, the famous border family and, as a child, delighted in stories of border raids. He would often go walking and climbing in Northumberland with his father.

Bunting attended the Royal Grammar School in Newcastle and Quaker schools in Berkshire and Yorkshire, where he first stayed with a friend at Brigflatts (now in Cumbria). This place later became central to his vision as a poet of Northumbria.

Arrested as a conscientious objector in 1918, he was kept in the notorious Newcastle Guardroom, and later in Wormwood Scrubs. By 1923 he was in Paris and had met Ezra Pound, who dedicated his *Guide to Kulchur* jointly to Bunting and Louis Zukofsky. He also worked for Ford Madox Ford on the *Transatlantic Review*. He followed Pound to Rapallo, later meeting W. B. Yeats, who termed him 'one of Pound's more savage disciples'. Poverty, however, was a constant pressure on Bunting, driving him to a multitude of shifts in order to live – barman, road-digger, artist's model, boat skipper, *Times* correspondent and a spell as a music critic. Other feats included riding a motorbike to the top of Mount Etna and, while living in the Canary Islands, beating the local military governor, General Franco, at chess.

During World War II, Bunting had a vastly varied experience, serving in Iran and North Africa and rising to the rank of Squadron Leader. By 1951, some of his poetry had been published but, as a supposed modernist, he was out of fashion in Britain. He struggled to make ends meet, living at various times in Throckley, and 'Shadingfield' cottage in Wylam, where Judge Drabble's talented family were neighbours for a time. After the break-up of his marriage, he moved into a Northern Arts rented council flat in Washington

New Town. He spent many years there up to the late 70s, but by 1981 he had moved to Greystead, near Bellingham. His final place of residence was Fox Cottage, Whitley Chapel, Slaley. For much of this time, he was working for the *Newcastle Evening Chronicle*, sub-editing the financial page, forgotten as a writer.

The local poet, Tom Pickard, eventually persuaded him to write again, and the result was his quasi-autobiographical masterpiece *Briggflatts* (so spelled) first read in the Morden Tower on the mediaeval walls of Newcastle.

Robert Burns (1759–1796)

The celebrated Scottish poet recalled that one of the formative influences on his talent was a book of ballads collected by Joseph Ritson, the Stockton-born antiquarian. He carried it in his pocket while at his work as a plough-boy.

Burns made a trip through the Border country in 1787, crossing the Tweed at Coldstream. This part of Northumberland pleased him, it seems, but though Berwick is described by Sir Nikolaus Pevsner as one of the most exciting towns in England, Burns was unimpressed by it and its people.

Later on his journey, Burns wrote a letter to Robert Ainslie from Newcastle on 25 May, complaining about his uninspiring travelling companions.

Josephine Butler (1828–1906)

Josephine Butler, the great social reformer, was born in Milfield, though the family moved to Dilston when she was seven. She was educated mainly at home and recalls attending the annual County Ball in Alnwick with great pleasure.

She began her work for destitute women and prostitutes in Liverpool in 1866, and pressed for educational and employment opportunities for women, editing *Woman's Work and Woman's Culture*, a collection of essays, in 1869.

Her greatest efforts were directed against the Contagious Diseases Acts and she wrote many books and pamphlets in support of the cause. After the repeal of the acts, she established and edited her own periodicals. Her account of the struggle was entitled *Personal Reminiscences of a Great Crusade* (1896).

In addition, she wrote biographies of Catherine of Siena, and Jean Frederic Oberlin, as well as of her father John Grey of Dilston, the radical agricultural reformer, of her husband, George Butler, the churchman and educationalist, and her sister Harriet.

Josephine Butler is buried at St Gregory's in Kirknewton.

Lord Byron (1788–1824)

Deep in the plantations off the road to the right from New Pittington to Easington Lane, stands Elemore Hall, the birthplace of Annabella Milbanke, wife of Lord Byron. The family home was Seaham Hall (put to various uses since) and was Annabella's home when she married Lord Byron there in January 1815. The drawing-room where the ceremony took place still exists, but has none of the original furnishings.

Byron was at Seaham on 13 November 1814 when, in a letter, he expresses his persistent doubts over marrying Annabella. She had turned him down before and Byron seems to hope for the like again. He always speaks rather distantly of Annabella to his friends, and his praise has an unenthusiastic air of duty about it. There is usually a touch of mockery in his description of her virtues or talents; her interest in mathematics caused him to dub her his 'Princess of Parallelograms'.

After the honeymoon at Halnaby Hall, Sir Ralph Milbanke's house just across the Tees in North Yorkshire, Byron was more relaxed back at Seaham among company (he got on well with his mother-in-law). Soon, however, he seems to feel trapped again; walks to Featherbed Rocks begin to pall. Of Seaham, he says in a letter of February 1815:

> Upon this dreary coast, we have nothing but county meetings and shipwrecks: and I have this day dined upon fish, which probably dined upon the crews of several colliers lost in the late gales. But I saw the sea once more in all the glories of surf and foam . . .

The marriage had lasted a year, when Annabella left him on grounds of cruelty, and incest with his half-sister Augusta. The character of Donna Inez in Byron's great comic masterpiece *Don Juan* is based on Annabella, as are Miss Millpond and Aurora Raby.

Caedmon (fl. AD 670–680)

Caedmon is the earliest English Christian poet, the 'Father of English Song'. He is the first English poet we know by name, just as Bede is the first prose writer. According to Bede, Caedmon was a servant at the monastery at Whitby, who received the gift of song in a vision. 'Thus sang he of the creation of the world, and the beginning of the race of men, and all the history of Genesis . . . also of the terrors of the future judgment and the horrors of hell-punishment and the sweetness of the heavenly kingdom.'

This short 'Hymn of Creation' quoted by Bede, the only work that can certainly be attributed to Caedmon, is in the Northumbrian dialect.

William Camden (1551–1623)

The great Elizabethan antiquary and historian, praised by the poet Edmund Spenser as 'the nurse of antiquity/ And lantern unto late succeeding age,' was born in London, though his mother's family (Curzon) was from Cumberland.

Camden's famous work *Britannia* (1586) is based on his travels round England during his holidays as a Westminster schoolmaster. An enlarged and improved version of *Britannia* came out in 1607: the book is written in elegant Latin, and was first translated in 1610.

Camden called the Cheviots 'lean, hungry and waste,' just as Leland before him, in the 1530s, had referred to 'craggi and stoni montanes'. Camden found the Borderers just as hard and describes them spearing fish on horseback in the Solway. He visited the Roman Wall in 1599 and though he could not get as close as he wished because of 'the rank robbers thereabout', he writes in admiration:

> Within two furlongs of Carvoran on a pretty high hill the Wall is still standing, fifteen feet in height and nine in breadth . . . Verily

I have seene the tract of it over the high pitches and steepe descent of hilles, wonderfully rising and falling.

Lewis Carroll (1832–1898)

Charles Lutwidge Dodgson (who wrote as Lewis Carroll) moved with his family from Cheshire, where Charles had been born in 1832, to the vicarage at Croft, near Darlington, in 1843. It remained the family home until 1868. Charles attended school in nearby Richmond for some two years (1844–46) before moving on to Rugby. At this time he used to write stories and poems, and invent games for the entertainment of the numerous family at Croft, where the large shady garden remains much as the Dodgson children knew it.

One of his many amusing early poems begins:

> Fair stands the ancient Rectory,
> The Rectory of Croft,
> The sun shines bright upon it,
> The breezes whisper soft.
>
> From all the house and garden,
> Its inhabitants come forth,
> And muster in the road without,
> And pace in twos and threes about,
> The children of the North.

Carroll also wrote a humorous ghost story called 'The Legend of Scotland', referring to the part of Auckland Castle where Scottish prisoners were once kept. The story, set in 1325, involves Bishop Bek of Durham, so that Carroll can bring in one of his puns as the joke ending. Carroll was a keen photographer and a comical story 'A Photographer's Day Out' was published in the *South Shields Amateur Magazine* in 1860. In the first surviving diary of his early manhood, we find that he met 'three nice little children' belonging to a Mrs Crawshay in Tynemouth in 1855.

Most of his famous poem 'Jabberwocky' which begins:

> 'Twas brillig and the slithey toves
> Did gyre and gimble in the wabe

was written on a visit to his Wilcox cousins in Whitburn, near Sunderland in 1855. Mrs Wilcox was the wife of the Collector of Customs in Sunderland; their house, High Croft, was later burned down. The 'beamish' in the line: 'Come to my arms my beamish boy!' is assumed to be taken from the Durham village.

Carroll probably also composed 'The Walrus and the Carpenter' while walking on Whitburn and Seaburn beaches. The distinctive headgear of a ship's carpenter was a common sight in a great ship-building centre like Sunderland. The walrus once kept in Sunderland Museum, however, arrived later – and has now disintegrated except for the head. Carroll's connection with Whitburn is commemorated by a statue in Cornthwaite Park.

Sid Chaplin (1916–1986)

Sid Chaplin was born at 23 Bolckow Street, Shildon, and worked as a miner until 1946. While living at 9 Gladstone Terrace in Ferryhill, he published his first masterly collection of stories, *The Leaping Lad* (1946), which was set in the County Durham mining villages. It gained him a prize which enabled him to take a year off and produce his first novel, *My Fate Cries Out*, about the lead miners of Weardale. Sid Chaplin can be said to have influenced a whole generation of post-war British writers, including Keith Waterhouse and Stan Barstow.

He also helped to form Northern Arts, this country's second Regional Arts Association. Based in Newcastle, it was founded in 1961. Meanwhile, his 1950 novel *The Thin Seam* and other stories formed the basis for a successful and moving musical play, *Close the Coalhouse Door*, by Alan Plater and Alex Glasgow.

From 1957, Chaplin lived at 11 Kimberley Gardens in Sandyford, Newcastle. Remarking that the term 'regional writer' made him spit blood, he wrote television scripts, including some for *When the Boat Comes In*. His two important novels, *The Day of the Sardine* and *The Watcher and the Watched* are set among the working class communities of Scotswood, Byker and Elswick, while his late stories included in *On Christmas Day in the Morning* (1978) and *The Bachelor Uncle* (1980) mark a return to the coalfield villages of County Durham, a milieu in which he was unmatched.

John Cleveland (1613–1658)

Cleveland, 'the last of the Metaphysicals', was the most popular poet of his age (far more so than Milton, for example) and 25 editions appeared between 1647 and 1700. His reputation declined, however, after Dryden's criticism that the poet was apt to deliver 'common thoughts in abstruse words.' His often dazzling conceits and comparisons were termed 'Clevelandism'.

Cleveland was an ardent Royalist during the Civil War and served as judge advocate at Newark, where King Charles I surrendered to the Scots in 1646. Charles was taken to Newcastle, and a plaque in Market Street indicates the house where the king was held for some eight months of tense bargaining, until the Scots, much to Cleveland's disgust, handed him over to Parliament. One of his most savage satires, 'The Rebel Scot' was written on this occasion.

Cleveland seems to have been a destitute wanderer between 1646 and 1655, dependent on Royalist sympathisers for support. His actual whereabouts, however, are a mystery. It is not impossible that he was in the North East for some of this period, and the poem 'News from Newcastle' (first printed in 1651) is ascribed to him. It certainly has more of Clevelandism than other poems so ascribed, and whoever wrote it was a poet of more than usual accomplishment. He clearly also knew the Tyne (and possibly Cleveland's work) very well. The beginning is arresting – and Newcastle is pronounced Geordie fashion:

> England's a perfect world, has Indies too;
> Correct your maps, Newcastle is Peru!

Then follows a wonderfully convoluted set of conceits in praise of coal. The poet mentions 'the bald parched hills that circumscribe our Tyne' and with surprising fervour, now writing as if he were a Tynesider, mentions Blaydon and Stella, as he sees London's wealth draining northwards:

We shall exhaust their chamber and devour
Their treasures of Guildhall, the Mint, the Tower.
Our staiths their mortgaged streets will soon divide,
Blathon own Cornhill, Stella share Cheapside.

William Cobbett (1763–1835)

Self-taught, Cobbett was a master of what Hazlitt called 'plain, broad downright English'; indeed he is one of the great prose writers in the language. He had pioneered what is now *Hansard*, and his celebrated *Rural Rides* combines keen observation with witty, energetic writing on agricultural themes. Though no revolutionary, he often savaged the government for corruption and incompetence.

This fiercely independent radical largely confined his activities to southern counties, but he did eventually come north in 1832, and his observations on farming in Durham are of great interest. He considered that the cattle were by far the most handsome he had ever seen. He was clearly out of his depth in the colliery districts, however, where some Geordie wag must have encouraged him to believe that miners and their families lived underground all their lives!

A deputation waited on him in Newcastle on 21 September 1832, with an address. Much moved, Cobbett exclaimed that after thirty years of attacks 'from the poisonous mouths and pens of three hundred mercenary villains, called newspaper editors and reporters' and twice being stripped of his earnings, put in jail and driven into exile: 'Here I am on a spot within a hundred miles of which I never was before in my life; and here I am receiving the unsolicited applause of men amongst the most intelligent in the whole kingdom.'

He lectured in South Shields on 2 October, crossing the Tyne to North Shields at eleven o'clock at night and made a very firm bargain with himself 'never to do the like again.' After lecturing in North Shields on 3 October, Cobbett travelled to Sunderland via Newcastle the next day. En route, he visited the prominent Newcastle citizen Armorer Donkin, on the lip of Jesmond Dene. Donkin had laid out a plantation six years previously, in the way advocated in Cobbett's *Woodlands*, and the author had requested to see it. Donkin also gave him a copy of Bewick's *Fables* and showed him a portrait of the artist, whom Cobbett greatly admired.

Of Sunderland, Cobbett wrote on 4 October 1832:

The pitmen have twenty four shillings a week; they live rent-free, their fuel costs them nothing, and their doctor costs them nothing. Their work is terrible to be sure; and, perhaps, they do not have what they ought to have; but at any rate, they live well, their houses are good and their furniture good; and though they live not in a beautiful scene, they are in the scene where they were born and their lives seem to be as good as that of the working part of mankind can reasonably expect.

Cobbett calls Newcastle 'this fine, opulent, solid, beautiful and important town' and lectured there on the evening of 5 October 1832. He then travelled to Hexham via Morpeth. The fertility of the Tyne valley round Hexham pleased him greatly, and he noticed that the biennial stocks stood the winter without any covering, 'which, as everyone knows, is by no means the case even at Kensington or Fulham.'

In Hexham, he attacked the prominent local citizen and politician, Thomas Wentworth Beaumont, who had annoyed Cobbett with talk that people disapproved of Cobbett as much as they detested the Tories. Cobbett quotes Swift, who said that if a flea or a bug bit him, he would kill it if he could. 'And, acting upon that principle, I, being at Hexham, put my foot upon this contemptible creeping thing, who is offering himself as a candidate for the southern division of the county, being so eminently fitted to be a maker of the laws!'

Cobbett was particularly delighted at the absence of potatoes in prosperous Tynedale – 'a certain sign that the working people do not live like hogs . . . From this degrading curse the county of Northumberland is yet happily free!'

Catharine Cockburn (1679–1749)

Born Catharine Trotter of Scottish stock, she was initially a dramatist, though she had a novel and verse in print by the time she was 14. Probably out of need, she wrote moralising tragedies like *Agnes de Castro*, acted at Drury Lane in 1695, when she was only 15 and *Fatal Friendship* (1698). A didactic comedy *Love at a Loss* was acted in 1700.

She published work defending John Locke's philosophy in 1702 (and 1726) and corresponded with Leibnitz, Congreve and Farquar. She also published a theological *Discourse* in 1707. In 1708, she married the Rev. Patrick Cockburn and bade 'adieu to the muses', living 'in a manner dead' till her children grew up. Cockburn was episcopal minister in Aberdeen and vicar of Longhorsley in Northumberland, where the couple seem to have lived at least from 1737 to 1749, and possiby earlier. Catharine published ethical treatises in 1743 and 1747. Her collected prose works were published in 1751.

Samuel Taylor Coleridge (1772–1834)

In 1799, Coleridge and Wordsworth stayed at Thomas Hutchinson's farm on the Tees at Sockburn, near Darlington. There both of them fell in love, Coleridge with Sara Hutchinson, and Wordsworth with her sister, Mary, whom he married in 1802.

It was at Sockburn that Coleridge wrote his ballad-poem 'Love' addressed to Sara ('Asra'). The armed knight referred to is the mailed figure on the Conyers tomb in ruined Sockburn church. This figure has a wyvern at his feet, a reference to the Sockburn worm slain by Sir John Conyers centuries before and supposedly buried under the rock in the nearby pasture; this was the 'greystone' of Coleridge's first draft, later transformed into a 'mount'. The wyvern appears as a lamia, a female figure of destruction, and the poem was a direct inspiration for John Keats' celebrated 'La Belle Dame Sans Merci'.

The Conyers falchion used to be ceremonially presented to each incoming bishop of Durham as he rode across the Tees at Croft, and can be seen at Durham Cathedral.

Later, Sara Hutchinson moved to a farm in Bishop Middleham with her brother George, and Coleridge was staying with them when he visited Durham on 25 July 1801, ostensibly to study Leibnitz in the Dean and Chapter Library. His request was taken to be 'live nits', according to the poet, and he was referred to a microscope-maker in the city.

Wilkie Collins (1824–1889)

Collins travelled round the North East on a theatrical tour with Dickens, and wrote numerous articles and stories for the latter's magazines. In 1861, he was in Whitby accompanied by Caroline Graves, the inspiration for *The Woman in White*. He was actually working on his novel *No Name*, but was driven away by the noise of children and brass bands outside his hotel.

The setting for his famous detective novel *The Moonstone* (1868) is 'high up on the Yorkshire coast', referring to the map rather than the elevation. Whether the genesis of the novel, with its fabulous diamond, mysterious Indians and Holmes-like detective, Sergeant Cuff, can be linked to the prominent presence in the area of the Maharajah Duleepsingh, is a matter of conjecture. The Maharajah, a favourite of Queen Victoria, had been deprived of the Koh-i-Noor diamond by the British in India. Based at Mulgrave Castle, he was a keen hunter (and cormorant-fisher) on the North York Moors, and was often to be seen there with his native retinue between 1859 and 1863.

Various guesses have been made as to the whereabouts of the Verinder house and lonely bay, locating it anywhere between Whitby and Middlesbrough.

Jack Common (1903–1968)

A plaque on 44 Third Avenue, in Heaton, Newcastle, marks the house where Jack Common, friend and correspondent of George Orwell, was born, close to the rail-sheds where his father worked as an engine-driver. In *Kiddar's Luck* (1951) Common vividly describes the life of the streets in Edwardian Tyneside, as seen through the lens of his adult socialism. Though *The Ampersand* (1954) took the story further, Common was unable to make a career in writing and died in poverty in 1968, leaving a mass of unpublished material, now held in the library of the University of Newcastle.

In 1928, Common had begun working for *The Adelphi* magazine in London and his articles appeared in many other periodicals. The essays collected in, for example, *Freedom of the Streets*, are a continual spur to thought with their wry humanity and quirky style: 'We begin with a handshake – now be ready to duck,' is how he ends his preface. Although he saw Orwell as a sheep in wolf's clothing (in pubs the barmen always called Orwell 'sir') the two remained friends. A curious fact is that Common modelled the brow for the well-known bust of Karl Marx in Highgate cemetery in London.

Joseph Conrad (1857–1924)

Barely a month after reaching England, Conrad had signed on for the first of six voyages, between July and September 1878, from Lowestoft to Newcastle, on a coaster misleadingly named *Skimmer of the Sea*. Crucially for his future career, he 'began to learn English from East Coast chaps, each built to last for ever and coloured like a Christmas card.'

In London, on 21 September 1881, Conrad set sail for Newcastle as second mate on the small vessel *Palestine* to pick up a cargo of 'West Hartley' coal bound for Bangkok. From the outset, things went wrong. A gale hampered progress (sixteen days to the Tyne), then the *Palestine* had to wait a month for a berth – and was finally rammed by a steam vessel. The captain's wife, Mrs Beard, looked after Conrad and sewed his buttons on, while he lived on board, moored not far from Percy Main.

The Beards lived in Colchester, and Conrad saw Mrs Beard off from Newcastle Central in a third-class carriage just before the *Palestine* sailed from the Tyne. Then the ship sprang a leak in the Channel and was stuck in Falmouth for a further nine months. After all these misfortunes, Conrad writes: 'Poor old Captain Beard looked like the ghost of a Geordie skipper.' Finally, off Java Head, the cargo ignited and fire engulfed the ship; the crew, including Conrad, reached shore safely in open boats. The ship is renamed the *Judea* in Conrad's story 'Youth', which is based on this episode, though he makes it rather more dramatic than it actually was. That voyage from the Tyne was Conrad's first fateful contact with the exotic East, the setting for many of his later celebrated works.

The great novelist's connection with the North East did not end there. In 1891, he stepped down in rank to sail as first mate on the famously swift passenger clipper, the 'wonderful' *Torrens*, quite possibly the finest ship ever launched from a Sunderland yard (James Laing's Deptford Yard, 1875). Conrad made two voyages to Australia aboard her, but by 1894 he had parted from the sea for ever and embarked upon his literary career – having begun writing his first novel *Almayer's Folly* on board the *Torrens*.

Archibald Joseph Cronin (1896–1981)

Cronin appears to have served as medical officer of health for Northumberland in 1921, and certainly travelled the country a good deal at this period as a medical inspector of mines. He wrote two books on mining safety, and was in Newcastle in 1924 in connection with the Montagu pit disaster, near Scotswood. Here, water from the Tyne had broken into the workings – an idea Cronin was to utilise in his first real triumph as a novelist, *The Stars Look Down* (1935). This is partly set in a mining community on the Northumberland coast ('Sleescale') and partly in Newcastle ('Tynecastle').

Cronin mentions a vast profusion of real Newcastle places – streets, shops, pubs, 'Esmond Dene' – and 117A Scotswood Road (spelt Scottswood, suggesting Cronin was going by memory, not just studying a map). The countless details of 1920s' Geordie life, colours, smells and all, fairly leap off the page. His portrait of Tynesiders is unpatronisingly sympathetic and he conveys the accent convincingly. Cronin also mentions Whitley Bay, Cullercoats, 'Sluice Dene', the River Wansbeck, and Tynemouth. Cronin's description of Newcastle celebrates the city Geordies then knew:

Tynecastle, that keen bustling city of the North, full of movement and clamour and brisk grey colour, echoing to the clang of trams, the clatter of feet, the beat of shipyard hammers, had engulfed Joe graciously . . . Joe had seen the gallery of the Empire, the inside of

Lowe's bar . . . Down the Scottswood [sic] Road he went, past the wide iron pens of the cattle-market, past the Duke of Cumberland, past Plummer Street and Elswick East Terrace . . . Joe had a stimulating sense of life around him and within him, he felt the world like a great big football at his feet and lustily prepared to boot it.

John Cunningham (1729–1773)

In the churchyard of St John's in Newcastle stands the table-tomb of John Cunningham, author of the play, *Love in a Mist*. He is described as a pastoral poet in this least pastoral of settings. Though of Irish-Scots extraction, he regarded Newcastle as his home. After many wanderings as an indifferent actor, he came back here to write poetry and end his days in 1773. Though much of his poetry has a gentle charm, he can show enthusiasm (and an Irish accent) in 'Newcastle Beer'.

The God of revelry on Olympus celebrates Britain's success in war:

> And freely declared there was choice of good cheer
> > Yet vowed to his thinking,
> > For exquisite drinking,
> Their nectar was nothing to Newcastle beer.

The poem concludes:

> > Your spirits it raises,
> > It cures your diseases –
> There's freedom and health in our Newcastle beer.

Cynewulf (fl. ? AD 800–825)

Cynewulf is the only Old English poet known by name, of whom any undisputed writings are extant (rather than being quoted by others). Though details of his life are lacking, Cynewulf was probably a Northumbrian churchman born in the eighth century. Unlike Caedmon, the other principal early English poet, Cynewulf seems to have been a man of education, familiar with the Latin liturgy and literature of the church of his day. He wrote skilled and felicitous alliterative verse in the Northern dialect of Old English.

At one time or another, almost all the great Anglo-Saxon poems, including the noblest of all, 'The Dream of the Rood', and the celebrated Riddles in the *Exeter Book* have been attributed to Cynewulf. Some may indeed be by him, but nowadays it is thought that only four are certainly his. These are 'Elene' and 'The Fates of the Apostles' in the *Vercelli Book*, and 'The Ascension' and 'Juliana' in the *Exeter Book*. In all of these, Cynewulf's runic 'signature' is interwoven with the verse. The finest of these is thought to be 'Elene', which describes the finding of the true cross by the Empress Helena, mother of Constantine the Great.

The Dalziel Brothers

The father of the celebrated Dalziel brothers, Alexander Dalziel of Wooler (1781–1832), was something of an artist himself, and seven of his eight sons by Elizabeth Hills became artists by profession. Margaret Dalziel (1819–94) was also a skilled wood-engraver and assisted her brothers from 1851 onwards.

George (1815–1902), the senior of the brothers, was educated in Newcastle and went to London in 1835 to be apprenticed. Later he set up on his own and was soon joined by brother Edward (1817–1905), who entered into partnership with him as the Brothers Dalziel. Thomas (1823–1906), the best illustrator of the family, joined his elder brothers in 1860.

Between 1840 and 1850, the brothers obtained the engraving of the blocks for the early numbers of *Punch* and the *Illustrated London News*. They also engraved many drawings by William Harvey, Thomas Bewick's pupil, between 1839 and 1866 and were employed for the Abbotsford edition of Sir Walter Scott's *Waverley Novels*. Others indebted to their zeal and enterprise were Millais, Tenniel and George Du Maurier. They cut the illustrations to Edward Lear's *Book of Nonsense* (1862) and Lewis Carroll's *Alice in Wonderland* (1866) and *Through the Looking-Glass* (1872).

When the *Cornhill Magazine* was founded in 1859, the Brothers Dalziel were entrusted with the engraving of all the illustrations. For technical skill combined with initiative, there was no one to touch them. After 1880, however, photo-mechanical processes began to supersede the slower and more expensive methods of the wood-engraver, and the brothers turned more to the production of illustrated comic newspapers. Their work can be seen in the British Museum and the Victoria and Albert Museum in London.

Sarah Emily Davies (1830–1921)

Emily Davies, though born in Southampton, was the daughter of the rector of St Mary's, Gateshead. A block of flats now stands on Bensham Road where the old rectory was. Denied the university education her brothers had enjoyed, her thoughts turned to the improvement of opportunities for women in society and, following a visit to London, she set up a branch in Gateshead of the Society for the Employment of Women.

After her father's death in 1862, she moved to London, where, as well as editing the *English Woman's Journal* and the *Victoria Magazine* for a time, she campaigned with Elizabeth Garrett and others for women to be admitted to university and the medical profession. She published *The Higher Education of Women* in 1866 (reprinted 1988) and her essays are collected in *Thoughts on Some Questions Relating to Women, 1860–1908* (1910).

Though Emily Davies helped to organise the first Suffragette petition, her main efforts were in the educational field. She established a college in Hitchin, Herts, in 1867, and this moved to Cambridge some years later, becoming the famous Girton College.

Late in life, Emily Davies returned to the Suffragette cause, but recoiled from militant action. That gently-reared women could be moved to at least token violence is shown by Lady Constance Lytton's celebrated stone, thrown at Walter Runciman's car on 9 October, 1909. This was during the protests against Lloyd George at the Palace Theatre, on the corner of St Thomas Street and Haymarket in Newcastle. In her book *Prisons and Prisoners*, Lady Lytton gives a touching account of her subsequent time in Charlotte Square gaol in Newcastle. After a fifty-six hour hunger strike, she was released because of a heart condition, supposedly discovered by the prison doctor. This revealing incident was featured in the TV series *Shoulder to Shoulder*, though the action was transferred to London.

Daniel Defoe (1660?–1731)

Defoe was more interested in how people got their living than in describing buildings or natural wonders. On his celebrated tour of Great Britain, published in 1724–27, he says for example: 'Darlington . . . has nothing remarkable but dirt.' Durham is described without rapture, though the clergy live 'in all the magnificence and splendour imaginable'. He is moved to compassion, however, by a mining accident at Lumley Park, 'where three score poor people lost their lives in the pit'.

Defoe was impressed by Newcastle and its quays: 'Well wharf'd up and faced with free-stone . . . the longest and largest key for landing and loading goods that is to be seen in England, except for that at Yarmouth . . . and much longer than that at Bristol.' Defoe marvelled at the amount of coal shipped from the port, and concludes: 'They build ships here to perfection, I mean as to strength and firmness, and to bear the sea.'

Defoe had been active in Newcastle as a secret government agent since 29 September 1706, when he rode across the Tyne Bridge and got the price of a new horse out of John Bell, the Postmaster in Newcastle. The Post House stood at the south end of Bigg Market, adjoining Pudding Chare. Defoe was passing under the name of Alexander Goldsmith at the time and was sounding local opinion about the proposed union of England and Scotland. In 1710 Defoe was back, this time under the name of Claud Guilot. He spent a good deal of time in the area over the next two years and took lodgings in Hillgate, just across the river in Gateshead, where Geordie tradition has it that he wrote *Robinson Crusoe*. He is thought to have published through Joseph Button, a bookseller on Newcastle Bridge and to have collaborated with him on the *Newcastle Gazette*.

Joseph Dent (1849–1926)

Dent was born in Archer Street, Darlington, in 1849, the tenth child of a house-painter. In his memoirs, he describes how he joined a Mutual Improvement society attached to his local chapel; there he was given the subject of Dr Johnson to prepare. By the time he had finished reading Boswell's biography, Dent's destiny was settled. Literature became a kind of religion for him, and though he recognised that he himself could never be a writer, he would serve as a door-keeper of the Temple, as he put it.

In 1867, the apprentice book-binder came to London, but it was not until 1888 that he felt able to pursue his dream of publishing. His Temple Shakespeare was a great success, selling a quarter of a million copies annually to begin with. Dent also encouraged young illustrators of talent, like Rackham and Beardsley, and attracted prominent men of letters to be his collaborators.

In 1906 came the beginning of Everyman's Library, for which he is world-famous. The idea was to build up a great 'city of books' on popular lines – he never lost sight of readers who, like himself, had left school at 13 and needed cheap high-quality books ranging over the world's literature.

By 1956, title number 1000 was reached, still with the famous line from the play *Everyman* inside:

Everyman, I will go with thee and be thy guide.

Thomas Dibdin (1776–1847)

Dibdin was a noted bibliographer and librarian to Lord Spencer at Althorp. Among his lively works is the *Picturesque Tour in the Northern Counties of England* (1838). Of the great new covered markets in Newcastle, named after Richard Grainger, he writes:

Learn therefore, that there is here the LARGEST market-place in England: probably in Europe . . . The markets of Newcastle cover somewhat more than two acres . . . The roof is of wood, with pendant corbels: the sides are of substantial stone. The whole is lofty, capacious and calculated for every good service, as well as picturesque effect. At given stations, there are fountains of marble in the centre: of which the water, in warm weather, refrigerates and sweetens the whole atmosphere. It is a glorious vista – and was once occupied (on the opening of the markets 22 October 1835) by TWO THOUSAND GUESTS; irradiated by gas-light. 'Nothing has been seen like it (said my friend Mr Adamson) since the days of Belshazzar . . .'

Of the Tyne, Dibdin remarks impressively: 'Upon the breast of this river, not fewer than fifteen thousand vessels are known in the last year to have taken their departures.' The river was famed for salmon; Dibdin records that on 12 June 1755, some 2,400 fish were taken in the Tyne, and upwards of 2000 on 20 June 1758. Dibdin gives a graphic picture of what met his eyes as he travelled across the Tyne from Gateshead to Newcastle in 1838:

Looking up to the County Hall, before you pendent from the clouds, with the old black castle . . . I have seen these objects lighted up by a setting sun, darting its beams of gold through a dense cloud of smoke, above which the summits of the two buildings glittered, as if they were not fastened down to the soil of this earth.

Of St Nicholas, however, he states: 'It is quite marvellous to consider what a fuss is made by the Newcastletonians about this, their "darling pet", as they call it.'

Charles Dickens (1812–1870)

Mr Wackford Squeers in *Nicholas Nickleby* is modelled on William Shaw, the former headmaster of Bowes Academy, which Dickens visited in the winter of 1837–38. His school (now flats) was the last building in the main street west of the village. A pump of the kind described by Dickens at Dotheboys Hall can still be seen through the courtyard.

Dickens and his illustrator Hablot Browne ('Phiz') stayed at the King's Head, Barnard Castle, and Dickens is said to have been influenced by the clock-maker's shop, then opposite the hotel, in choosing the title *Master Humphrey's Clock* (1840) for his new weekly in which *The Old Curiosity Shop* and *Barnaby Rudge* appeared.

Dickens acted in a bill of three plays at the Lyceum (large hall) in Lambton Street, Sunderland on 28 August 1852. Wilkie Collins also took part. The plays included Lytton's *Not so Bad as we Seem* and *Mr Nightingale's Diary*. According to Dickens, 'Little Darlington' had earlier covered itself with glory – unlike the disgraceful incident in 1841, when a drunk had offered the great Franz Liszt a sovereign to play 'God Save the Queen'. Durham had provided a 'capital audience'. After Sunderland, Dickens went on to appear on stage at the Old Assembly Rooms in Newcastle.

In Nelson Street in that city stands the Gaiety Theatre of 1838, where Dickens performed during his celebrated reading tours. These performances were not without their perils. On one occasion, during a gripping recital from *Oliver Twist*, the gas apparatus he used on stage to produce his lighting effects fell over. The author himself quelled an incipient panic. Dickens said of Newcastle's citizens: 'Although the people are individually rough, they are an unusually tender and sympathetic audience, while their comic perception is quite up to the high London average.' On another occasion he said: 'A finer audience there is not in England, and I suppose them to be a specially earnest people; for while they can laugh till they shake the roof, they have a very unusual sympathy with what is pathetic or passionate.'

Dickens also visited Tynemouth and wrote in a letter from Newcastle, dated 4 March 1867:

> We escaped to Tynemouth for a two hours' sea walk. There was a high north wind blowing, and a magnificent sea running. Large vessels were being towed in and out over the stormy bar with prodigious waves breaking on it; and, spanning the restless uproar of the waters, was a quiet rainbow of transcendent beauty. The scene was quite wonderful. We were in the full enjoyment of it when a heavy sea caught us, knocked us over, and in a moment drenched us and filled even our pockets.

Another curious Dickens echo is found in Northumberland. At seventeen, he had become infatuated with Maria Sarah Beadnell, the daughter of a London banker, and remained besotted with her for two years. In 1845, however, she married Henry Louis Winter, a Finsbury sawmill manager. After Winter went bankrupt in 1859, he became vicar of Alnmouth. The young Maria is the model for Dora Spenlow in *David Copperfield*.

In late 1861, Dickens gave a reading at Berwick on Tweed, a fact commemorated by a plaque on the outside of the King's Arms Hotel.

Thomas Doubleday (1790–1870)

Born in Newcastle, Doubleday early adopted the views of William Cobbett, and was a political supporter of Earl Grey of Fallodon and the Whigs. He was prominent in the agitation leading up to the Reform Act of 1832.

Doubleday eventually succeeded his father George as partner in a soap manufacturing firm in Newcastle, which eventually failed. Possibly this was partly due to Doubleday's absorption in literature. In 1832 he had published an *Essay on Mundane Moral Government* and, in 1842, attacked the ideas of Malthus in his *True Law of*

Population. He published a biography of Sir Robert Peel in 1856 and a financial history of England since 1688.

Doubleday contributed to *Blackwoods Magazine* and the *Manchester Guardian*, as well as the *Newcastle Chronicle*. He also penned a Venetian romance, *The Eve of St Mark's*, as well as a number of plays. The last of these, *Caius Marius*, was written at the suggestion of the great actor Edmund Kean, whose eventual verdict, however, was discouraging.

Doubleday's *Collection of Coquetdale Fishery Songs* appears to be written in Lowland Scots for some reason, but his keen interest in the North East heritage is demonstrated by *A Letter to the Duke of Northumberland on the Ancient Music of Northumberland, its Collection and Preservation.*

Thomas Drayton (1563–1631)
The prolific poet, Shakespeare's contemporary, gives a rather superficial enumeration of many North East locations, in his most ambitious project, the long topographical work *Poly-Olbion*. Of Newcastle, he writes:

> That place no lesse is fam'd
> Than India for her Mynes . . .

John Duns Scotus (1265–1308)
'Doctor Subtilis', the greatest English mediaeval philosopher, is commonly said to have been born in Duns, Berwickshire, just over the Northumberland border, but Dunstan near Craster also has its claim. As for 'Scotus', one should remember that the notion of Scotland as being anywhere north of York is of considerable antiquity! At all events, there is a strong tradition that Scotus entered the monastery of the Grey Friars in Newcastle around 1280. This lay at the top of Grey and Pilgrim Streets.

His later lecturing and writing career in Paris, Oxford and Cologne, saw his doctrines emerge as an alternative system to that of St. Thomas Aquinas, and his influence has been strong up to the present day. His followers were sometimes derided as 'Dunsmen' or 'Dunces', a word that has found its uses in subsequent ages.

John Bacchus Dykes (1823–1876)
Born in Hull, he was appointed precentor at Durham Cathedral in 1849 and bought 'a very pretty little cottage . . . about a mile out of Durham, with a nice little bit of garden and a very fine prospect.' This was Hollingside Cottage, where he lived until September 1853. One of his most celebrated hymn-tunes is called 'Hollingside', after the cottage, which lies on Hollingside Lane, off South Road.

Hearing of plans to issue *Hymns Ancient and Modern*, Dykes sent seven hymns he had written himself and which had been popular locally. The music editor accepted all of them and eventually no fewer than 60 of Dykes' compositions were included in the first edition of 1861. He is regarded as being among the great hymn-writers and several of his creations continue in general use, including – 'Holy, holy, holy', 'Jesu, lover of my soul,' 'Eternal Father, strong to save,' and 'Nearer my God to thee'. He died at 53, and is buried in St Oswald's churchyard.

José Maria Eça de Queirós (1843–1900)
Portugal's greatest novelist worked in the consular service at 53 Grey Street in Newcastle, from late 1874 until April 1879. These years were among the most productive of his career. Among his celebrated novels, he published the second version of *O Crime de Padre Amaro* (1876), and *O Primo Bazilio* (1878), as well as working on a number of other projects including his fifteen 'Cartas de Londres' for a Portuguese newspaper. He even mentions the title of his masterpiece *Os Maias* in 1878, though this was largely written during his residence in Bristol.

Elizabeth Elstob (1683–1756)
'The Saxon Nymph' was born and brought up in the Quayside area of Newcastle, and, like Mary Astell, is nowadays honoured as being one of the first feminists in England. She was proficient in eight languages and became a pioneer in Anglo-Saxon studies, an unprecedented thing for a woman.

In London, she translated Madeleine de Scudery's *Essay upon Glory* in 1708 and *English-Saxon Homily on the Nativity of St Gregory* in 1709. Both works are dedicated to Queen Anne, who is praised in feminist prefaces. From 1702 onwards, Elizabeth was part of the circle of intelligent women around Mary Astell, who helped to find subscribers for her *Rudiments of Grammar for the English-Saxon . . . with an Apology for the study of Northern Antiquities* (1715), the first ever such work. In it, Elizabeth took issue with and probably influenced the formidable Jonathan Swift.

Her brother William Elstob (1673–1715) was sent to Eton and Cambridge and entered the church. Like his sister, he was a scholar and edited Roger Ascham's *Letters* in 1703. Elizabeth may have lived with him at Oxford from 1696 and certainly did so in London from 1702.

Elizabeth Elstob, like her mother Jane, was a keen admirer of feminine learning and kept lists of famous women. In middle age, however, a school she was running in Evesham failed because she was inadequate at spinning and knitting! She eventually secured an apartment, where she lived 'surrounded by the congenial elements of dirt and books', until she died in 1756.

Eric Bloodaxe (d. AD 954)
The greatest Saxon king, Athelstan, the conqueror of Northumbria, is also the subject of the first royal portrait we possess. He is shown symbolically handing a book to Saint Cuthbert. In AD 934, Athelstan prayed in Chester-le-Street for Cuthbert's aid in his forthcoming expedition to Scotland, placing various items in the saint's coffin, including the eastern silks which can still be seen in Durham Cathedral.

The Northumbrians, notably Archbishop Wulfstan of York, a resolute northerner, chafed under the domination of the hated *Suthangli*. Though they had submitted to Athelstan's son, Eadred, in AD 947, they took the opportunity of asserting their independence by inviting the charismatic Eric Bloodaxe to be king in York. The most celebrated Viking of his era, Eric had briefly been king of Norway. His own saga is, unfortunately, lost, but others survive to testify entertainingly, if unreliably, to his prowess.

Literary works written in the north of England in the tenth century include the *Life of Saint Oswald*, which tells of the Northumbrian king and martyr, who defeated the heathen Welsh king Cadwallon at Heavenfield, near Hexham, in AD 634. It should also be remembered that there were a number of chronicles compiled in the north, which, though lost, are being slowly disentangled from the compilations of later writers. These annals and genealogies, ending with the *History of the Earls* in the eleventh century, look back with nostalgia on the last flicker of Northumbria's greatness, which Eric's time represented. Like Athelstan, Eric had journeyed to Chester-le-Street to visit the shrine of St Cuthbert, and in the *Liber Vitae* of the community, his name is still to be seen.

Roger of Wendover, the chronicler, in his *Flores Historiarum*, quotes an English churchman, writing in York soon after AD 954: 'Eric Bloodaxe was treacherously slain . . . in a certain lonely place which is called Stainmore . . . betrayed by Earl Oswulf [of Bamburgh].' It appears that Roger had been relying on the work of a Northumbrian historian, now lost. As Michael Wood remarks, 'If only we possessed it today!'

The modern road between Brough and Bowes follows the Roman road, the one Eric Bloodaxe took that day in AD 954. High in the sweeping moorland, at the old frontier of Northumbria, stands the stump of the Rey Cross, from the Norse *hreyrr*, meaning 'boundary'. It has been suggested that this may even have been an English wheel-cross erected in memory of Eric. Though Eric had been baptised as a Christian in England, the poem *Eiriksmal*, commissioned by Eric's widow, depicts the Norse hero arriving at Valhalla straight from Stainmore and being warmly welcomed by Odin.

Basil Bunting's great poem *Briggflatts* contains the lines:

> Bloodaxe, king of York,
> king of Dublin, king of Orkney.
> Take no notice of tears;
> letter the stone to stand
> over love laid aside lest
> insufferable happiness impede
> flight to Stainmore . . .

Eric was the last king of an independent Northumbria. John of Wallingford's *Chronicle* states: 'From that time to the present, Northumbria has been grieving for want of a king of its own, and for the liberty they once enjoyed.' The lost *History of the Ancient Northumbrians* ended with Eric's death and concluded: 'Ever since, the Northumbrians have been mourning their lost liberty.'

John Meade Falkner (1858–1932)

Born in Wiltshire, Falkner had originally come to Newcastle, after Oxford, to be tutor to the children of Sir Andrew Noble. He became an intimate and beloved figure in Jesmond Dene House and gradually rose to the top of the Armstrong-Whitworth firm by 1916 – hard though this is to equate with his poetry and his interest in heraldry and architecture. He wrote several novels, including *The Nebuly Coat*, which has been seen as influencing E. M. Forster. His great claim to fame is the children's classic *Moonfleet* (1898), several times dramatised, filmed and televised. Some consider it to be more enjoyable than *Treasure Island*.

Falkner was captivated by Durham, and after becoming honorary librarian to the Dean and Chapter, lived in the Divinity House on Palace Green from 1902. A plaque there commemorates his residence, and his monument is in the South Cloister of the cathedral.

Celia Fiennes (1662–1741)
The travels of Celia Fiennes are a delight to read, as much for her wayward spelling as for her racy and vivid descriptions of late seventeenth century England. To journey round the country side-saddle was in itself something of a feat, and her book is deservedly a classic. She considered that Newcastle 'most resembles London of any place in England . . .' She remarks that 'there is another pyasoe with brickwork pillars at the Holy Jesus Hospital.' Next door, in the Barber Surgeons Hall she admired the pretty garden and also the anatomised bodies:

> One, the bones were fastened with wires the other had the flesh boyled off and some of the ligeaments remained and dryed with it . . .; over this was another roome in which the skin of a man that was taken off after he was dead and dressed and so was stuff'd the body and limbs, it look'd and felt like a sort of parchment . . .

She then coolly comments on the fine view to be had from this room.

Like Defoe some years later, she admired the Newcastle Quayside, and thought the shops good and the markets cheap. She describes in her inimitable style, 'little things look black on the outside and soft sower things.' What she meant by these curious items of Geordie cuisine, we may only conjecture.

Ford Madox Ford (1873–1939)
Ignoring Violet Hunt's strong opposition, Ford had enlisted in the army in 1915, despite being over age at 42, and was commissioned in the Welsh Regiment. He had two spells of duty in France but was invalided home for good on 15 March 1917. In early January 1918, he was moved to a training appointment in Redcar. Violet joined him, but relations became very strained. On one occasion she scratched his face so badly that he had to go on sick leave rather than face the regiment!

Ford in turn recorded his own feelings about some of these events in his great *Parade's End* tetralogy, where Violet is portrayed as Sylvia Tietjens. In March 1918, he was attached to the staff and went all over the North of England lecturing on the Ross rifle, and the causes of the war.

Stella Bowen, whom Ford had met that spring, came to see him at Redcar in October 1918 and they watched what they thought was the last convoy to France sail out of Tees Bay. Stella also came to Redcar for his birthday on 17 December.

Ford, by now a captain, was gazetted out of the army on 1 January

1919, rather disgruntled and suspicious that he had not been asked to stay on as education adviser to Northern Command with the rank of lieutenant colonel. London had become a strange city to him, after his experience of the war. He mentions that the shouts of the railway porters, 'London only!' at Ashford, Exeter and (significantly) Darlington, would no longer apply to him.

His war tetralogy *Parade's End* has a Yorkshire squire as hero, with his manor house at 'Groby'. This is actually Busby Hall, Carlton-in-Cleveland, the residence of Arthur Marwood (1868–1916), who had founded the *English Review* with Ford in 1908. Marwood was a cousin of Lewis Carroll and an accomplished mathematician. He is the model for Christopher Tietjens in *Parade's End* as his brother, Sir William Marwood (1863–1935) is the model for Mark Tietjens.

Edwin Morgan Forster (1879–1970)

Forster's Uncle Willie was a huntin', fishin' and shootin' gentleman, who lived at Acton House, near Felton in Northumberland. Forster stayed with him for a part of the summer for several years around 1900. He wrote a letter from there on 27 July 1899, describing a trip to 'Bamborough'. He examined the Forster tombs, deciding that Bamburgh was such an appropriate cradle for the family that he would always consider these Forsters his own ancestors – the coat of arms was certainly close to his own. He goes on: 'I paddled on the deserted beach and felt very Calibanish for I had nothing to dry my toes with and the sand stuck them together.'

Forster was certainly at his uncle's in April 1904 and writes from there again on 28 October 1905. At some point after this, relations with the unpredictable Uncle Willie broke down and Forster came no more.

Acton House is an impressive two-storied ashlared building of about 1780 and Forster, by his own account, used it as the model for Cadover, in his own favourite novel *The Longest Journey* (1907). This was Forster's most autobiographical work, in which, also by his own account, the character of Mrs Failing owes much to Uncle Willie.

On 22 July 1914, Forster was staying at Duns in Berwickshire and mentions a visit to the Turners, where he met Ford Madox Ford. He describes Ford, at forty, as 'flyblown' and very bored. This was the house party which was expecting the arrival of the young Wyndham Lewis.

John Forster (1812–1876)

In a now-demolished part of Fenkle Street, Newcastle, John Forster was born on 2 April 1812. He also lived in Low Friar Street close by. Forster, educated at the Royal Grammar School, had a play performed (for one night) at the Theatre Royal in 1828. Later on, in London, he became an important journalist and editor, associating with the leading literary folk of the day. He was a friend of Mrs Gaskell and persuaded her to entitle her famous novel *Mary Barton*, rather than use the name of John Barton, the murderer. He also persuaded Tennyson to restore the lines, 'Half a league, half a league/ Half a league onward . . .' to the beginning of 'The Charge of the Light Brigade'.

From 1837, he read in manuscript everything that Dickens wrote, and left these priceless documents to the nation when he died. Forster is recognised as the first professional biographer in nineteenth century England, and his life of Dickens in three volumes (1872–74) is regarded as a standard work over a century later. Dickens described Forster's London home as Mr Tulkinghorn's residence in *Bleak House* and immortalised his pompous but lovable friend as Mr Podsnap in *Our Mutual Friend*.

George Fox (1624–1691)

Just above the Royal Arcade (now replaced by Bank House) on Pilgrim Street in Newcastle, once stood the Friend's Meeting House, together with its burial ground. The door and pediment now adorn the new Meeting House in Jesmond Road. George Fox, the founder of the Society of Friends, or Quakers, came to Newcastle from Scotland in 1657, and in his *Journal* records a different reception from that which John Wesley was to get.

Fox's movement often suffered ill-usage from crowds at this time and Fox himself was imprisoned four times during the Cromwellian period. Across the Tyne, Gateshead was more accommodating than Newcastle, where the Quakers used to meet in the open air near the Moot Hall. The Friends' redoubtable foe in Newcastle was Alderman Ledger, to use Fox's spelling. Ledger sneered memorably that 'the Quakers would not come into any great town, but lived on the fells like butterflies.' Fox, no doubt leather-clad as always, read him a lecture. In the *Journal*, Fox rejoices that these magistrates were turned out in 1660 'when the king came in'.

Samuel Garth (1661–1719)

Born in Bolam, near Bishop Auckland, Garth studied medicine and eventually became physician to King George I, and physician-general to the army. He was knighted in 1714.

In 1697 Garth delivered the Harveian lecture, in which he advocated a scheme to provide dispensaries for the poor, as a protection against the greed of chemists. He also moved in literary circles and became a member of the celebrated Kit-Cat Club. His mock-heroic poem 'The Dispensary' (1699) returns to the theme of his lecture, and ridicules apothecaries and their allies among the doctors. The poem proves that the heroic couplet could be written with smooth elegance even before the days of Alexander Pope.

He wrote little else besides 'Claremont' (1715), a moralising topographical poem in the manner of Pope. He did, however, translate part of Dryden's Plutarch, as well as editing and part-translating a composite edition of Ovid's *Metamorphoses*, published in 1717. Garth was a free-thinker, but his friend Pope called him 'the best good Christian without knowing it'.

Elizabeth Gaskell (1810–1865)

Elizabeth Stevenson, as she then was, high-spirited and handsome, came to Newcastle and stayed for the winters of 1829 and 1830 with her relation, the Reverend William Turner at 248 Westgate Road (then 13 Cumberland Row). Her father, incidentally, had been born in Berwick upon Tweed.

Turner was a Unitarian minister who served the Hanover Square congregation for 59 years, until his retirement at 80. One of the founders of the Literary and Philosophical Society in 1793, he was said to have been active in 'every benevolent and scientific interest in the town'. George Stephenson was his pupil and never forgot the help he had received.

There is no doubt that Turner's social, practical Christianity appealed to Elizabeth Stevenson's compassion and sense of justice. This side of her is very much in evidence in novels like *Mary Barton* and the controversial *Ruth*, her 'Newcastle novel', as she called it. It seems probable that Turner's daughter, Ann, was the model for Faith Benson in that book, and the Reverend Thurston Benson may well be based on William Turner. Like him, he is a Unitarian pastor, a man of rare goodness, charm and active charity during the Hungry Forties.

Elizabeth left the Turner household in April or May 1831, and it was in December of that year that the great cholera epidemic spread to Newcastle. Interestingly, the celebrated John Snow was working in the area as a colliery surgeon during the epidemic, having been apprenticed to the Newcastle doctor, William Hardcastle. In 1849, he famously demonstrated that cholera was waterborne. The Soho pub which stands on the site of the pump which Snow identified as the source of the cholera outbreak there is now called after him.

It is hard to say to what extent the Eccleston or Fordham mentioned in *Ruth* refer to Newcastle, but certainly Ruth goes to St Nicholas Church and walks home through 'The Leasowes' (Leazes?). At all events, the Turner house is described in the novel, and the climax of the book is the cholera epidemic. Turner had remained in the city to assist in the relief work and, as an old man in Manchester, related his personal memories to Elizabeth, now Mrs Gaskell. The inadequacy of the relief measures and the lack of nurses figure vividly in the novel's pages.

It has often been observed how advanced were Mrs Gaskell's attitudes to poor relief and to Ruth herself, a 'fallen woman'. These attitudes, however, are still rather more Victorian than a modern reader finds comfortable. Nevertheless, the book created a storm of controversy when it appeared in 1853 and some circulating libraries banned it. It has been pointed out that the characters in Dickens' *Hard Times*, published a year later, bear some similarity to those of *Ruth*. Elizabeth Barrett Browning also admired *Ruth*, and her novel in verse, *Aurora Leigh*, has noticeable echoes of Mrs Gaskell's 'Newcastle novel'.

A pleasant touch about Geordie speech comes from Mrs Gaskell's letter to Miss Fox in 1849: 'I picked up quantities of charming expressive words in canny New Castle . . .'

It is clear from a letter that the young Elizabeth Stevenson enjoyed Newcastle: she had many friends there and went dancing (possibly in the Old Assembly Rooms). The well-known bust of Elizabeth, by the younger David Dunbar, was probably done in the city. It is also just possible that Tynemouth is echoed in the 'Abermouth' of the novel; several episodes are set there, including the poignant scene where Ruth rejects the shallow Mr Bellingham on the sands.

Certainly Elizabeth knew the coast here well; the dashing harpooner, Charley Kinraid, one of the chief characters in her Whitby novel *Sylvia's Lovers* (1863) comes from Cullercoats and has a Northumbrian burr in his voice. 'Singing hinnies' (Northumbrian scones) are mentioned as a speciality of northern housewives, and there are also many knowledgable references to (North) Shields and Newcastle in the first half of the book.

'Robinson, Side, Newcastle' is an establishment where information about new agricultural machinery can be garnered. New Gate and Broad Chare are also mentioned. Even the Whitby church is called St Nicholas, not St Mary's. At a dramatic part of the narrative. Kinraid sings 'Weel may the keel row' in the streets of Acre in Palestine.

Wilfrid Gibson (1878–1962)

Gibson was born on Battle Hill, in Hexham, though only the room above the archway next to the post office remains. He wrote the lines for the fountain erected in the market place in 1901. Despite the fact that he went to London in 1912, and later lived there and in Gloucestershire, many of Gibson's poems both then and later are set in rural Northumberland and deal with poverty and passion amid wild landscapes. Others are devoted to fishermen, industrial workers and miners, often alluding to local ballads and the rich folk-song heritage of the North East. Though occasionally powerful, they are often conventionally melodramatic and do not convince nowadays, despite all the Northumbrian names they use. Gibson must be the only poet to set a dialogue on Bloodybush Edge.

His war poems are more immediate and every schoolchild used to know his 'Flannan Isle' about the three lighthouse keepers, mysteriously missing. Gibson was published in Edward Marsh's *Georgian Poetry* and was a friend of Rupert Brooke, who made him one of his heirs.

Philip Larkin, while compiling the *Oxford Book of Twentieth Century Verse*, complained of the poets he had to read through, and decided that Gibson had never written a good poem in his life. He eventually included no fewer than six Gibson poems all the same. Gibson's work influenced the early Auden and he could certainly produce thrilling effects on occasion, as in the opening stanza of 'Lindisfarne':

> Jet-black the crags of False Emmanuel Head
> Against the winter sunset: standing stark
> Within the short sun's frosty glare, night-dark
> A solitary monk with arms outspread
> . . . .
> With drooping head he seems to hang in air
> Crucified on a wheel of blood-red fire.

Penelope Conner Gilliatt (1932–1993)

Penelope Gilliatt, though born in London, was brought up in Northumberland. Her father, Cyril Conner, was Director of the BBC in the North East from 1938 to 1941, and Penelope and her sister, now a noted sculptress, seem to have lived at Farnley Farm, a mile south east of Corbridge.

Throughout her distinguished career as a writer and film critic in

London and New York (she won an Oscar nomination with the screenplay for *Sunday, Bloody Sunday* in 1971), Penelope retained a love of the Roman Wall country.

Her novel *Mortal Matters* (1983) is largely set in Northumberland and Newcastle, mentioning the Old Assembly Rooms, the Grainger Market, Grey Street and much else. She celebrates the achievements of the North East and writes a good deal about, for example, the famous vessels *Mauretania* and *Turbinia* – indeed the south of England (exemplified in Harrow and the Stock Exchange) is portrayed as a sybaritic and corrupting influence. There are several loving pages devoted to Hexham, and the North East is held up throughout the book as a model of acumen and courage. Braw Fell is clearly Cragside, and the master, Sir William Douglass, is obviously modelled on Lord Armstrong. Douglass was the family name of Penelope's mother Mary.

Godric (1065?–1170)

Born in Norfolk, Godric was a much-travelled trader (called 'a pirate' by a contemporary chronicler). In 1102, he assisted King Baldwin I of Jerusalem to escape after the battle of Ramleh and also made many pilgrimages around Europe.

In middle age, he settled down for a time with an old recluse near Bishop Auckland, but from 1110 to the end of his long life, he lived in a hut at Finchale, near Durham. He was a strongly-built man with long hair and blue eyes and, according to Reginald of Durham, was painfully aware that his early life had been disreputable. He sought to make amends as a hermit. His self-mortification was grim and his reputation as a seer grew: he even had power over snakes, which he treated as pets.

Bearing in mind that the last dateable poem in Old English (AD 1104) is about Durham City, it is very remarkable that the earliest examples known of native popular verse in Middle English have been preserved by Godric's biographers. This makes him the earliest known lyrical poet in English altogether. The first of these four pieces, 'Cantus Beati Godrici' is an eight-line poem asking the Virgin for help in attaining heavenly bliss. Godric's dead sister is supposed to have given him a four-line hymn, while the third poem 'Cantus Sancto Nicholao' was inspired by an Easter vision of the patron saint of seafarers. Not only that, the extant melodies of these hymns are ascribed to Godric as well, which would make him the author of the earliest known musical settings of English words.

Oliver Goldsmith (?1730–1774)

Goldsmith spent two weeks late in 1753 in the Newgate gaol, then part of the Newcastle town wall, where Newgate Street meets Gallowgate. According to his own account, the ship on which the luckless poet was sailing to the continent was driven by a storm into the Tyne and the authorities held him on suspicion of travelling to join the French army. Goldsmith writes: '. . . as we were all very merry, the room door bursts open, enters a sergeant and twelve grenadiers and puts us all under the king's arrest . . . I endeavoured all I could to prove my innocence; however I remained in prison with the rest a fortnight, and with difficulty got off even then.'

It may well be that the prison scenes in *The Vicar of Wakefield* owe something to this uncomfortable experience – though the Newgate gaol was very well appointed as prisons went and was praised by prison reformers. On the other hand, some have accused the poet of romancing over this episode; the ship which Goldsmith said had gone down with all hands off Bordeaux has not been traced. It has been suggested that Goldsmith was actually unromantically jailed in Sunderland for debt.

Jane Gomeldon (d. 1780)

The Feminist Companion to Literature in English states that Jane Middleton, well educated in languages, science and philosophy, was married at an early age to Captain Francis Gomeldon, a friend of George Bowes, the Newcastle coal magnate. She left him, however, and escaped to France in male dress, where a number of exploits are ascribed to her. She returned to England on Gomeldon's death in 1751.

Her book of 31 essays, *The Medley*, published in Newcastle in 1766, raised over £53 for the city's lying-in hospital. In the essays, Jane assumes a male persona to discuss Milton, Homer, the education of daughters, cross-dressing, and the unbroached subject of female adultery – having resolved 'not to play the Prude'. She asserts that gentlemen now need improvement to render them fit to be companions to women. She cites Richardson and the courtesan Teresa Constantia Phillips, and creates a range of lively fictive characters.

Her *Maxims*, published in Newcastle in 1779, puts traditional wisdom into irregular verse. The *Companion* gives a reference to P. M. Horsley in *Heaton Works Journal*, 6, 1951.

Thomas Gray (1716–1771)

The celebrated poet and scholar is one of the best letter-writers in the language. He used to visit his friend, Dr Thomas Wharton at Old Park, a farm on the Wilmington road, 3 miles north-east of Bishop Auckland. Wharton's experimental farm and gardens were an attraction for the tourist of his day.

Gray writes to Wharton on 26 August 1766 from the south coast:

> Whatever my pen may do, I am sure my thoughts expatiate nowhere oftener and with more pleasure than to Old Park . . . The coast is not like Hartlepool, there are no rocks, but only chalky cliffs of no great height, till you come to Dover . . .

On 21 June 1767, Gray writes:

> The Monday following we go to York to reside, and two or three days after set out for Old Park, where I shall remain upon your hands; and Mr Brown about the time of Durham races must go on to Gibside, and for aught I know to Glamis.

One letter, dated August 12th 1767, is headed Old Park, Nr Darlington, Durham. Another, to Wharton dated Dec. 28 1767 speaks of a certain cargo:

> . . . that I sent to Miss Wharton and Miss Peggy, directed to the former, to be left at Mr Tho. Wilkinson's in Durham. This went

by the Newcastle waggon about 6th of December, and contained twelve flower roots; viz, three Soleil d'or narcissus; two white Italian ditto (N.B. of the double white and yellow Italian there are none to be had this year); two pileus cardinalis, red; one kroonvogel; one degeraad, double white; one Bella grisdelin; one hermaphrodite; and one incomparable, double, blue, hyacinth. For these you must get glasses from Newcastle.

Dora Greenwell (1821–1882)

The poet Dora Greenwell was born on 6 December 1821 at Greenwell Ford, near Lanchester. She was taught by a governess for five years, and then taught herself, studying philosophy, political economy and languages. After the loss of Greenwell Ford, the family moved to Ovingham, where Dora taught local girls, and published her *Poems* (1848).

In 1850, the family settled at Golbourne in Lancashire, where Dora became friendly with Josephine Butler and supported her work. After 1854, the Greenwells lived in Durham. This was the period of Dora Greenwell's greatest intellectual achievement, and she met many literary celebrities, including Jean Ingelow and Christina Rossetti. After 1874, she settled in London and supported the franchise struggle. She also became addicted to opium.

Dora Greenwell's poetry, as exemplified in *Carmina Crucis* (1869), *Songs of Salvation* (1873) and other works, is marked by intense religious feeling. She has been compared to Christina Rossetti.

Her prose works include *The Patience of Hope (1860), Two Friends, Essays* (1866) and *Colloquia Crucis* (1868). The essay 'Our Single Women' is a plea for a broader education of intelligent women.

Ivor Gurney (1890–1937)

After being gassed during service on the western front, Gurney was sent back to England in 1917. Reluctant to return to France, he went on a four-month signals course in Northumberland, billeted most probably in Gloucester Terrace, New Hartley, near Seaton Delaval. The terrace had indeed been named for the regiment at the beginning of the war and still stands behind the club in the tiny village.

In a letter of 17 November to Winifred Chapman, Gurney says: 'This place is a pit village, ugly enough, but the (rather tame) sea is only four miles away, and the wind roars continually.' The November weather was inclement. He continued to write poetry at Seaton Delaval, however, including the one beginning: 'Lying awake in the ward', published in *War Embers*. As a pianist and song-writer (his songs were occasionally being performed in London at this time) he also vamped accompaniment at a parish concert ('Some concert! but they were very pleased').

Gurney had been invited out to tea on 23 December and, though he pined for his native Gloucestershire (rather unfairly comparing the spring and autumn evenings there with winter in the Northumberland coalfield), he found that 'the people are kind, which makes up for a lot'.

In a letter to Marion Scott of 10 January 1918, he complains of his quarters being a 'freezing, ugly, uncomfortable Hell of a hole. The other men get round the fire and take the bench, one cannot write in the billet on the table therefore. Only warm weather or France will alter things.' He bought *More Soldier Songs* in Blyth, however, to inspire him (though on 20 January, he writes that he bought it in Newcastle).

A letter to Marion Scott of 25 February 1918, tells her that he had been for examination in Ward A 17, number 1 in the Newcastle General Hospital on Westgate Road. Not having expected to do more than report, the verdict depressed him and he took a ten minute walk into the city to pick up a Boswell and took comfort from it.

While convalescing, Gurney writes on 12 March 1918 from the Gallery Ward in Brancepeth Castle. He finished a number of songs at the castle, despite the piano sounding like 'a boiler factory in full swing because of the stone walls.' He was in better spirits, despite his health problems and a visit to Durham on 13 March 1918 left him awe-struck:

> To gaze on that magnificent group of buildings from across the river on the first day of spring! O but it was a revelation, a vision beyond price!

He writes again to Herbert Howells on 22 April 1918 from Ward A18 in Newcastle General Hospital: 'It is Sunday and all the shops are shut, which does not brighten canny Newcassel, where people have very kind hearts and very rough manners often. Very hospitable in a manner almost unknown in the South where they are poorer.' Another letter on 7 May, says that 'the weather has been beautiful . . . and Tyne Side has looked just like South Country. The sea in Whitley Bay was quite wonderful . . .'

Hadrian (AD 76–138)

The gifted Roman emperor made two great tours of his domains, during the first of which he visited Britain in AD 122. The emperor himself was out bare-headed in all weathers along his frontiers, and one contemporary writes: 'I wouldn't like to be the emperor as he does his British walkabouts!' (or words to that effect).

His mighty defensive wall is now a World Heritage site, like Durham Cathedral and Castle. Hadrian gave the bridge and settlement on the Tyne his own family name – Pons Aelius. It lay roughly where the castle keep is now. The Swing Bridge is on the site of the Roman crossing.

The artistic emperor was a middling poet himself – his inspired death-bed poem which begins 'Animula, vagula, blandula' is one of the most celebrated in antiquity.

John Hardyng, (1378–?1465)

The chronicler John Hardyng was a member of Hotspur's household and witnessed the battle of Homildon Hill near Wooler in 1402, where Hotspur and the Earl of March overcame the Scots under Douglas. He was also present when Hotspur met his death at Battlefield (still so called) near Shrewsbury in 1403. Hardyng later became Constable of Warkworth Castle and served under Hotspur's conqueror, now Henry V, in the war against the French. His rhymed history of England, *The Chronicle of John Hardyng*, is in feeble verse and of interest chiefly for the eye-witness account of Agincourt.

Hardying was a prudent man. The original chronicle had been Lancastrian in tone, and ended in 1436. The revised version supported the Yorkist cause and went on to 1461. This was the version he presented to Edward IV.

Augustus Hare (1834–1903)

Hare is the author of the longest autobiography in the world. The early volumes paint a picture of Victorian cruelty masquerading as religion more improbable than anything in Dickens.

Hare's first literary guide was so successful that he was asked to do more, and chose Northumberland and Durham. Hare used his widespread family connections to stay at the stately homes of the North East while doing his research, often based at Ridley Hall, near Riding Mill. He used to visit the Marchioness of Waterford at Ford Castle every year. Hare was in Newcastle on 6/7 May 1862, where he stayed with the Clayton family in Westgate House (now demolished) in Fenkle Street. On a visit to his clergyman friend, Edward Liddell, in Jarrow in 1876, Hare found him:

> Amidst a teeming population of blackened, foul-mouthed, drunken rogues, living in rows of dismal houses, in a country where every vestige of vegetation is killed by noxious chemical vapours, on the edge of a slimy marsh, with a distance of inky sky, and the furnesses vomitting forth volumes of blackened smoke. All nature seemed parched and writhing under the pollution . . .

More characteristic of Hare, however, are the entrancing descriptions of Teesdale, the Otterburn Moors, Gibside, Ridley Hall, Falloden and Rock, Dunstanburgh and Holy Island. A description of Chillingham Castle, where Hare stayed with the Tankervilles can stand for them all:

> This park is quite as beautiful in its way as any scenery abroad and much more so, I think, than any in Scotland. It is backed by the Cheviot Hills and often broken into deep dells, with little streamlets running down them, and weird old oaks whose withered branches are never cut off, sheltering herds of deer. Great herds too of wild cattle which are milk-white, and have lived here undisturbed since time immemorial, come rushing every now and then down the hillsides like an army to seek better pasture in the valley . . . Nothing can be more lovely than the evening effects each day I have been here, the setting sun pouring streams of golden light into the great grey mysterious basin of the Cheviots, amid which Marmion died and Paulinus baptised the ancient Northumbrians.

Hare knew Algernon Swinburne and Wallington Hall, where the unpredictable Sir Walter Trevelyan had him served a meal consisting entirely of artichokes and cauliflowers. A great teller of stories, Hare's extraordinary account of the man who kept marrying women with wooden legs is perhaps the most entertaining, while the tale of the Croglin Grange vampire can still make the flesh creep. Of Wallington Hall, he writes:

> Wallington is still a haunted house: awful noises are heard all through the night; footsteps rush up and down the untrodden pas-

sages; wings flap and beat against the windows; bodiless people unpack and put away their things all night long and invisible beings are felt to breathe over you as you lie in bed.

Jane Harvey (1776–1842)

According to the *Feminist Companion to Literature in English*, Jane Harvey was the daughter of Elizabeth and Lawrance Harvey of Barnard Castle. She published by subscription in Newcastle a *Sentimental Tour* of that city as by 'a Young Lady', in 1794, with sections like 'The Theatre Royal', 'Merchant's Court', and 'Tea' with lively talk on politics and women.

Her *Poems on Various Subjects*, 1797 was followed by some dozen anonymous novels, mostly, but not all, published in London. These are competent works, rich in unusual detail. *Minerva Castle*, 1802, and others were published by Minerva. *The Castle of Tynemouth*, 1806, is a tale of alleged witchcraft set in the fifteenth century.

Jane Harvey also wrote verse and tales for children, ending her creative career in 1841 with *Fugitive Pieces*, an intriguing mixture of charming poetry, political support for striking Tyneside keelmen and exploited female tailors, a witty welcome to 'the railroad', and an elegiac 'Conclusion'.

Jane was probably related to the Margaret Harvey, who ran a boarding school in Bishopwearmouth and published a long poem and melodrama (1814, 1822) on the history of the Percy family in the sixteenth century.

Nathaniel Hawthorne (1804–1864)

The celebrated American author came to Redcar (from Whitby) on 26 July 1859, in search of peace and quiet as he worked on the final draft of *The Marble Faun*. He stayed until early October before moving to Leamington to complete the 508 page manuscript, which was not completed until 8 November. Hawthorne's house in Redcar stands at the junction of High Street and King Street in the middle of the town. Formerly the Hawthorne Café, the premises at the time of writing belong to the furniture retailers Homestart.

Harold Heslop (1898–1983)

Heslop was born in New Hunwick, near Bishop Auckland, and later worked for many years at Harton Colliery in South Shields, where he lived with the Gibsons at 23 Marsden Street and, after his marriage, at 1 Gorse Avenue in Cleadon.

Heslop's literary output included a crime novel praised by Dorothy L. Sayers, but was largely based on his experiences in the mines and associated union activity in the coalfield. He was cited by Sid Chaplin as a formative influence (alongside D. H. Lawrence), but though *Last Cage Down* (1935) was a critical success, his usual fate was to have much of his output rejected.

In the USSR however, Heslop was promoted as a proletarian writer of whom much was expected. He was the only British writer invited to speak at the International Conference of Revolutionary and Proletarian Writers in Kharkov in 1930, and his impressions of the USSR, his attendance at a show trial, and an extraordinary interview with Yevgeni Zamyatin, who tried out his Geordie accent, are never less than absorbing. The strength of his autobiography *Out of the Old Earth*, published by Bloodaxe, however, lies in his rich recollections of childhood in the coalfield and the fine descriptions of working life underground.

Heslop's work may be seen as part of the long and impressive North East tradition of coalfield writing. In particular, songs of mining life and 'pit poetry', whether humorous or pathetic, are an integral part of the region's heritage. The celebrated 'Collier's Wedding' was written by Edward Chicken, clerk of St John's Church in Newcastle for 25 years, and buried there in 1746. Thomas Wilson who wrote 'Pitman's Pay', worked for the firm of Losh, Wilson and Bell. Joseph Skipsey, treated below, was a working miner who achieved national notice, while Wilfrid Gibson constantly used mining themes and imagery.

Outsiders too, like A. J. Cronin in *The Stars Look Down*, or James Henry in his savagely bitter poem on the Hartley disaster of 1862, which begins: 'Two hundred men and eighteen killed', have sought subject matter in the great coalfield. Auden's fine poem 'O lurcher-loving collier, black as night' is from the film documentary *Coal Face* (1935).

Ralph Hodgson (1871–1962)

Hodgson was born in Garden Street, Darlington, the son of a coal merchant. He ran away from school and spent much time in the south of England, working as an artist in London in the 1890s. His poems were published in *Georgian Poetry* and in three short collections, of which *Poems* (1917) made his name.

Hodgson is best noted for his nature poems, in which he railed against man's cruelty to animals. These include the much anthologised 'The Bells of Heaven', 'Stupidity Street' and, perhaps most notably 'To Deck a Woman'.

Thomas Jefferson Hogg (1792–1862)

Hogg was born at Norton House in Norton, and attended Durham school, before leaving for Oxford in 1810. He was a friend of Shelley at University College and collaborated with the poet on 'Posthumous Fragments of Margaret Nicholson'. He also took part in alarming scientific experiments which stained Shelley's hands and clothing with chemicals. When Shelley was sent down for writing *The Necessity for Atheism*, Hogg refused to deny complicity and was expelled with him.

Hogg urged Shelley to marry the 16-year old Harriet Westbrook in 1811, the world not yet being ready for the rejection of marriage as an institution. Nevertheless Shelley cooled towards him in 1812, when Hogg took too close an interest in Harriet. The friendship was renewed the following year. Hogg meanwhile published a romance, *Memoirs of Prince Alexey Haimatoff*.

Hogg became a barrister and eventually inherited £2000 under Shelley's will. In 1855 he began to write the poet's biography, but Shelley's family denied him further access to papers after the first two volumes turned out to be more about Hogg than Shelley.

Ernest William Hornung (1866–1921)

The celebrated creator of Raffles was born at Eardley Villa, Grove

Hill, Middlesbrough, though house and road have now disappeared under the Grove Hill estate. His father was a coal exporter and also served as the Swedish, Norwegian and Danish vice consul. His premises were in Turton Street (also gone).

Young Hornung was sent to Uppingham public school, after which he joined the family business. He then spent two years in Australia (1884–86), apparently for health reasons. That country forms the background for several of his works. He worked as a journalist and married Sir Arthur Conan Doyle's sister in 1893. As if to counter Sherlock Holmes, Hornung invented the gentleman-thief A. J. Raffles, whose exploits are recounted by his faithful friend Bunny. Conan Doyle disapproved of casting a criminal in the role of hero, while Hornung for his part made outrageous puns at Holmes' expense – Raffles remarks that 'though he might be more humble, there's no police like Holmes'. The first Raffles book *The Amateur Cracksman* appeared in 1899. Raffles was successfully dramatised and has been played on the screen by Ronald Colman and David Niven among others.

George Orwell regarded both the Sherlock Holmes and Raffles stories as enjoyable examples of the 'good bad' book, which would survive when more earnest authors had been forgotten. Orwell considered Hornung a very able writer on that level and one of his most celebrated essays is entitled 'Raffles and Miss Blandish'.

Violet Hunt (1862–1942)

The notorious 'new woman' novelist, sometimes dubbed 'Violent Hunt', was born in Durham at 29 Old Elvet. Her parents had earlier lived at Crook Hall (where John Ruskin came to stay) about a mile from the cathedral. Her father, Alfred Hunt, was a painter of pre-Raphaelite leanings, with a passion for the wild landscapes of Northumberland.

Violet's mother, Margaret, wrote many lightweight novels with happy endings and had begun taking drawing lessons in Durham from William Bell Scott in 1851, when she was twenty. It was through Scott that she learned of Rossetti and the Pre-Raphaelites, who were to loom so large in her life – and indeed through him that she had met her future husband. The Hunts moved to London in 1865, when Violet was three, partly in order to further Hunt's career, partly because of friction with the Durham clergy, whom Margaret was to picture unflatteringly in her first novel *Magdalen Wyngard*.

Violet later wrote seventeen novels, all concerned with sexual politics and relationships. While her parents were alive, the family spent many holidays in northern England and kept up the connection with Ruskin in the Lake District. Her novel *The Human Interest* is set in the same locations, notably by the River Greta, as is *Magdalen Wyngard*.

Violet Hunt's writing is curiously neglected today, but in her time she was admired by many, including Henry James, D. H. Lawrence, Rebecca West and May Sinclair. She had several well-publicised affairs, including, inevitably, H. G. Wells, and more surprisingly, Somerset Maugham. From another liaison she contracted syphilis. Violet was the model for Norah Nesbit in Maugham's *Of Human Bondage* (1915), but she was less pleased when he dedicated his travel book *The Land of the Blessed Virgin* to her. That seemed inappropriate.

Between 1908–1918, she conducted a stormy liaison with Ford Madox Ford and appears as Sylvia Tietjens in Ford's great war tetralogy *Parade's End*.

Aldous Huxley (1894–1963)
On 10 October 1930, Huxley delivered a lecture at Willington on the theme of science and literature. This visit to Durham made a considerable impression on him, according to his most recent biographer, D. Bradshaw.

Certainly, Huxley was moved to reflect on the fact that though his Willington hosts were kind and intelligent, he himself felt more at home with a member of the Durham Cathedral clergy, a man of similar background to his own. Huxley concluded that the public school system was responsible, and remarked that 'we' took good care to maintain this and other barriers. His tone is rueful and resigned rather than complacent or supercilious. One feels that Huxley, despite his remoteness from the world of manual labour, is actually more perceptive than Priestley in this area.

Bradshaw states that Huxley first went down a mine on 19 February 1931, probably the Brancepeth 'C' pit at Willington. He was greatly struck by the beauty of the miners' bodies, almost defenceless, it seemed, in the 'monstrous twilight' of the coal face. Conditions in the coalfield, however, appalled him. In a letter, he uses the word 'awful' to describe them, and indicates that his own honest reaction is to run away as far as possible. He felt that the situation was hopeless and that absolutely nothing could be done.

Huxley also visited Middlesbrough and was aware of the town's growth and significance. Like most literary intellectuals, however, he could not respond to the spectacle of heavy industry. Rather revealingly, he feels dwarfed by it. Though the great Transporter Bridge has been described by Sir Nikolaus Pevsner as a European monument, 'in its daring and finess, a thrill to see' Huxley doesn't mention it. His description of Durham Cathedral is also low-key. His poor eyesight may account for this, but can hardly explain his extraordinary assertion that he never saw a cabbage growing in the North East. He presumed that vegetables must be imported: the 'barriers' evidently prevented him from questioning the natives on the point.

Huxley's self-assurance as he pronounces upon what he only half-comprehends, speaks volumes about the gap between the social classes at this period. The title of the Willington article is, significantly, 'Abroad in England'; that on Middlesbrough speaks of 'alien Englands'.

William Earl Johns (1893–1968)
On 1 April 1918, the creator of 'Biggles' was appointed flying instructor at Marske in Cleveland. Aircraft were very unreliable in those days and he promptly wrote off three planes in three days due to engine failure – crashing into the sea, then the sand, and then through a brother officer's back door. Later he was caught in fog over the Tees, missed Hartlepool and narrowly escaped flying into a cliff. Shooting one's own propeller off with the synchronised

forward-mounted gun was a rare accident but it happened to Johns twice!

After the war, Johns worked in the RAF recruiting office in Newcastle. He arrived late on 31 December 1924 and spent a horrific night at 15 Ellison Place, then a disused private nursing home. His bed collapsed, leaving him entirely in the dark, without matches. He did however have the company of noisy rats, sounding as if they were wearing clogs, and intermittently biting pieces out of the floor. With a cheerfulness worthy of Biggles, Johns survived to serve a year in Newcastle, while living with Doris (Dol) Leigh, his devoted companion, on the coast at Whitley Bay. Johns began his writing career some seven years later. Unique among children's writers of the time, Johns employs a working-class character as an equal part of the Biggles team – Ginger Hebblethwaite, the son of a Durham miner.

Ben Jonson (1572–1637)
Though bulky and getting on in years, Jonson walked all the way to Scotland to visit William Drummond of Hawthornden, near Edinburgh. He passed through Newcastle on his way north in mid-August 1618, having bought a new pair of shoes in Darlington to replace those he had worn out: he was still wearing them when he came back through Newcastle in January 1619. John Taylor, the 'Water Poet', is thought to have burlesqued Jonson's enterprise in his own *Penniless Pilgrimage*, but Jonson, who met Taylor in Leith, good-naturedly gave him money to continue his journey.

Rudyard Kipling (1865–1936)
In India in 1886–88, Kipling knew the Northumberland Fusiliers best of all the British army regiments (he called them the 'Tyneside Tail-Twisters'). Bobby Wicks, the idealised young officer in the story 'Only a Subaltern' is drawn from the regiment.

In *Puck of Pook's Hill* (1906), there are three chapters devoted to a centurion of the (imaginary) 30th Legion, staunchly defending the Roman Wall in the days of the Empire's decline. The city Kipling mentions seems to be Corbridge. He cannot have been to the fort in Wallsend, as he describes it as 'Segedunum on the cold eastern beach'! His 'Roman Centurion's Song' is a plea to work in Britain and not be recalled to Rome:

> Some Western camp (I know the Pict) or granite border keep
> Mid seas of heather derelict, where our old messmates sleep.

For Kipling, the *Mauretania* was a mighty symbol. In 'The Secret of the Machines' (1911), he writes:

> The boat-express is waiting your command!
> You will find the 'Mauretania' at the quay,
> Till her captain turns the lever 'neath his hand
> And the monstrous nine-decked city goes to sea.

Lady Noble records that Kipling visited the Armstrong works in Elswick in February 1915, presumably in connection with his books *Fringes of the Fleet* and *The War at Sea* (1916).

John Knox (c 1513–1572)

Thomas Carlyle called Knox: 'The one Scotchman to whom of all others, his country and the world owe a debt.' By the time of his appointment in the Church of England to preach in Berwick, and later at St Nicholas Church in Newcastle, the turbulent priest had already seen his mentor John Wishart burned as a heretic by Cardinal Beaton in St Andrews, and, after joining the Cardinal's murderers in the castle there, had himself been captured by a French expedition and served nineteen months as a galley-slave. His discourse from the pulpit of St Nicholas on 4 April 1550 is one of only two examples of Knox's preaching style we possess. It is a tub-thumping display.

Knox seems to have resided on Castle Stairs, and Newcastle remained the fiery priest's headquarters until September 1552, when he moved for a time to London, before returning to St Nicholas to preach the Christmas sermon in December. Knox's first wife was Margaret Bowes, one of the fifteen children of Richard Bowes, the captain of Norham castle.

As king's chaplain, Knox had taken part, along with Nicholas Ridley, in King Edward VI's revision of the prayer-book. He denounced the execution of Lord Protector Somerset from St Nicholas pulpit in Newcastle in 1552. He was again in Newcastle in December 1553, after the accession of Mary Tudor, before prudently fleeing the country early the following year. Knox sent a number of propaganda tracts over from the continent and in one of them, in 1558, he expressed his frustration at the queens who had thwarted him – notably Mary Tudor and Mary of Guise, by publishing his celebrated *A First Blast of the Trumpet against the Monstrous Regiment of Women*. By regiment here, he meant rule. A ruling woman was, he said, 'repugnant to nature . . . the subversion of all equity and justice.' He had intended three blasts, but admitted that the first one had blown from him all his friends in England. Elizabeth I was, not surprisingly, greatly offended. Knox was also co-author of the *First Book of Discipline* (1559), which advocated a national system of education.

Knox became the leader of the Reformation in Scotland, of which movement he published a lengthy history in 1587. This includes his notable account of Mary, Queen of Scots' return to Scotland in 1561, his own interviews with her and his fierce denunciations from the pulpit of St Giles in Edinburgh.

Zamyatin's characters in *Islanders* spend an eventful evening on and around a mist-enshrouded Castle Stairs and King Street. Here Knox is surprisingly evoked as the ghostly 'Cobbler John', presumably because Castle Stairs was the centre of Newcastle's shoemaking trade in 1916. It prompts Zamyatin to muse briefly on Mary, Queen of Scots and the murder of Rizzio in Edinburgh, though he seems unaware of the plot's Newcastle connection.

Ebenezer Landells (1808–1860)

Landells, the son of a local merchant, was a favourite pupil of Bewick in the 1820s. He moved to London in 1829, where he established a high reputation as an engraver. He retained a great love for Newcastle as well as his Geordie accent, and was known as 'tooch-it-oop' to his affectionate staff.

It was Landells who originally thought up the idea of a London paper on the lines of Philippon's Paris *Charivari*. He submitted the idea to Henry Mayhew, and the first issue of the famous humorous magazine *Punch* came out on 17 July 1841. Noted literary men like Thomas Hood and William Thackeray became contributors, and Landells was the first engraver for the paper. Originally a radical and abrasive magazine, it gradually became less political. Tom Taylor, the Sunderland-born dramatist, was editor from 1874–80.

Philip Larkin (1922–1985)

Larkin dedicated *The Less Deceived* to Monica Jones, with whom he spent many holidays in the flat she owned at 1A Ratcliffe Road in Haydon Bridge (Monica's mother came from St John's Chapel in Weardale). Larkin was much taken by the fact that one of England's great rivers ran past the back of the property. He and Monica used to attend the spectacular New Year celebrations in Allendale, and was certainly there on New Year's Eve 1966 and again in 1970. He was, rather uncharacteristically, thrilled by it all.

His notable poem 'Show Saturday' (in the collection *High Windows* 1974) is a description of the 1973 Bellingham show, where Monica and he were regular visitors. They also spent much time driving round northern England and certainly crossed into Scotland at Carter Bar. Larkin also has some jocular lines in a letter, substituting Morpeth for Macbeth. Oddly, Larkin makes no mention of Auden's links with the North Pennines (and Bellingham), though he admired Auden to the extent of buying an Audi car in his honour.

Larkin thought well of Newcastle, and was there professionally in 1963 to study the lay-out of the university library.

Lawrence of Durham (d. 1154)

Lawrence was a Benedictine monk at Durham, who became Prior in 1147 and Bishop of Durham in 1153. He travelled to Rome for his consecration but died in France on his way home.

Lawrence was a pleasing poet who wrote in Latin. His *Hypnognosticon* is mainly a versification of scriptural material, but he also adds some poetic dialogue directed against the Scot, William Cumin, who had made tenacious attempts to take over the see of Durham on the death of Geoffrey Rufus in 1140, keeping out the next bishop for sixteen months. Lawrence's *Consolatio de Morte Amici* in mixed prose and verse, is in the manner of Boethius' celebrated sixth century *De Consolatione Philosophiae*.

Rosamond Lehmann (1903–1990)

Rosamond Lehmann, whose delicate, perceptive novels have been republished by Virago Press in recent years, married Leslie Runciman of the Tyneside shipping family, and son of the cabinet minister, in 1922. They lived in Newcastle close to the Great North Road near the university, at 3 Sydenham Terrace (now demolished). It was here that she began her best-selling first novel, *Dusty Answer* (1927), whose autobiographical background of Buckinghamshire and Cambridge helped to ease the strain of an unhappy relationship.

The aristocratic Rosamond, though beautiful and popular, with a fine house and servants, was uneasy in her middle-class Newcastle existence. Relations with her mother-in-law were strained, and not improved when Rosamond missed her cue during a pageant at Alnwick Castle organised by the older woman. Rosamond also found that her handsome, clever husband was cool towards women and had no desire for children. She eventually left him for the Hon Wogan Phillips (later Lord Milford), who had been living with the family while working in the Runciman firm. Phillips, incidentally, later became notorious as the only communist peer in the House of Lords. When he took his seat in 1963, his maiden speech proposed the abolition of the institution. He eventually left Rosamond at the time of the Spanish Civil War, for a more politically suitable partner.

Rosamond Lehmann's second novel, *A Note in Music* (1930), is dedicated to Phillips, and draws heavily on her Newcastle experience. Faced with adapting to a more provincial and practical milieu (the reverse of the usual situation in novels!), her response, as expressed through the main character Grace, is to retreat into complete inaction, passively observing the surface of things. 'Threadbare' is the key word in her one reference to the unemployed. Hugh Miller, the southerner working in the city, has social poise and grace of manner, conveyed here as moral qualities.

Rosamond Lehmann loads the dice heavily against Newcastle (unnamed). To allow the city any real attractions would clearly undermine Grace's rigidly aloof attitude: the bustling and characterful life of Newcastle and its people, therefore, is kept at an unsympathetic distance by giving the reader no familar warming reference. The city's history and handsome Regency townscape get no mention; even laburnum trees are somehow not genuine. Trams groan past (along Osborne Road) relentlessly throughout the novel. There are cinemas, theatres and lively night-spots, but none are named. Grace and Hugh jig to the latest dance-tune, but we do not discover what it is. There is no talk with ordinary Newcastle individuals (apart from servants). Crowds stare with a 'bulging, northern look'. On the tram they have blank faces.

Enjoyment at the Hoppings is left to the prostitute Pansy. Correct pleasure for Grace and her circle lies at a Georgian mansion in Northumberland (evidently Doxford Hall) with its bathing pool and tennis courts. The fear of spontaneous commitment outside her accepted code is almost alarming: Jane Austen herself could not be more fearful of the wilderness. When one thinks of Swinburne (a southerner) and his glad response to Northumberland, Grace's tone is plaintive indeed:

> 'I think if you're born and bred a southerner you never quite get used to the climate – or anything – here. You may get to love it, but it's almost like living abroad, I think . . . You want to go home.'

John Leland (c 1503–1552)

Leland, the first of modern English antiquaries, became the first and last King's Antiquary in 1533, and travelled the country retrieving ancient documents from monasteries and colleges. In 1547, Leland became insane, always a danger for obsessional compilers, and his work remained in note form only (published as the *Itinerary* in 1710–12). Nevertheless, it was an invaluable mine of information for later topographers and historians, like Holinshed and Camden. It was also drawn upon by Michael Drayton for his *Poly-Olbion*.

Leland made two journeys in the North East. On the first, he arrived in Durham from Bishop Auckland, but his descriptions of the castle and cathedral are rather dull. He spent most of his time in the cathedral library, which had ten long desks. The first three were devoted to the bible, the next three to religious texts; the seventh was for history, the classics and lives of saints; the eighth and ninth were for canon and civil law; the tenth was exclusively for Aristotle. In all, the library contained over 1,000 manuscripts and 500 printed books.

The Benedictine monastery at Durham had a great reputation for learning and was one of the richest in England at this time. It maintained its own college at Oxford (Durham College, later Trinity) and its own grammar school. It also possessed a mechanical clock.

The *Rites of Durham*, written by a lay servant at this time gives a good picture of the monastery in its last years. Though religious foundations were to be dissolved by Henry VIII, and they were under attack by Leland's Protestant contemporaries, the writer praises 'the goodly religious' for their humility and goodness.

Leland went on as far as Newcastle via Chester-le-Street ('chiefly one street of very mean buildings'). He remarks of the walls of Newcastle that in strength and magnificence they 'far passith all the waulls of the cities of England and most of the cities of Europe'. Two miles in extent, up to thirty feet high and studded with seventeen formidable towers, they were considered by experienced soldiers to be far stronger than those of York, and on a par with Avignon and Jerusalem. Newcastle still possesses more of its walls than all but four English cities.

On his second visit, in 1542, Leland rode the length of the Roman Wall, noting Lanercost Priory and inspecting the forts at Vindolanda and Housesteads. He crossed the North Tyne at Chesters and headed north towards Alnwick and Berwick via Newcastle. He speaks feelingly: 'Morpet, a market town, is XII long miles from Newcastle.' Nevertheless, he preferred it to Alnwick. Leland reached the Tweed at Carham, where he recalls a battle between the English and the Danes in AD 833, in which eleven bishops, two English counts and a great number of people were slain.

Whatever Henry VIII's real interest was in the project, Leland's noble and inspiring aim had been, as he put it at the end of his life, to 'open a window that the light shall be seen by the space of a whole thousand years'.

Percy Wyndham Lewis (1882–1957)

As a painter, the stature of Wyndham Lewis (he hated 'Percy'), seems secure. As to his literary reputation, he has been called the greatest English-language writer of the century. Anyone who has read the novels of this extraordinary man will easily see why such a view might be taken – and also why this is not the general opinion.

In the summer of 1914, Lewis stayed with the Turners at a house in Berwickshire, just over the Scottish border, where E. M. Forster had stayed earlier. Ford Madox Ford and Violet Hunt were among the guests, and there was much discussion of whether a Liberal government would declare war: Ford was darkly certain it would.

Lewis' autobiography *Blasting and Bombardiering* contrasts this talk of war, and the headlines in the London papers, with the peace of the Scottish countryside. There, posters for the MORPETH OLYMPIAD symbolise local concerns. Lewis appears to think that Morpeth is in Scotland. The event referred to was actually the Morpeth Olympic Games held between 1870 and 1958, at various venues in the town; one such is commemorated by Olympia Gardens. These games were usually held around the August Bank Holiday, as they were in 1914, before being suspended for the duration of the war.

Travelling south to London, Lewis recalls his train halting on a bridge in Newcastle, where a large gentleman with bellicose designs on 'the Kayser' got into his carriage and impressed Lewis unfavourably. Fortunately for local sensibilities, Lewis has him speaking in cockney. Newcastle itself had appeared as one of the ports to be 'blessed' in Lewis' invigorating magazine *Blast*.

Henry George Liddell (1811–1898)

Liddell was born at Binchester, near Bishop Auckland. He was a celebrated Greek scholar, and his great *Greek-English Lexicon*, which he compiled with Robert Scott, first appeared in 1843. It immediately became the standard work in its field. He also wrote a popular *History of Rome*.

He became Dean of Christ Church at Oxford in 1855 and it was for his daughter Alice that Lewis Carroll wrote *Alice in Wonderland*.

John Lilburne (c 1614–1657)

Colonel John Lilburne, known as 'Freeborn John' and 'Lilburne the Leveller', was the author of many pamphlets championing the common man. He is often said to have been born in Greenwich, but the likelihood is that it was in Sunderland in 1615. At all events, the Lilburne family were of County Durham origin and had a town house in Sunderland at 83 High Street East, which stood till 1819. The family were regarded as being chief magnates of the district and Lords Paramount of the Borough and Port of Sunderland.

In *Innocency and Truth Justified*, published in 1645, Lilburne says:

> I was brought up well-nigh ten years together in the best schools in the north – namely, at Auckland and Newcastle – in both which places I was not one of the dronesset schoolboys there . . . at Newcastle I did not only know but also was known of the principal men there.

Lilburne was brought before the Star Chamber in 1638 for printing an unlicensed book, whipped and put in prison. In *The Work of the Beast*, he writes of the barbarous treatment he endured. He joined the parliamentary forces in 1642 and rose to the rank of lieutenant-colonel. In 1645, however, he refused to take the covenant, left the army and began to voice his mistrust of its leaders, earning a spell in the Tower in 1648, before being tried and acquitted. He was also exiled for two years, but on his return courageously continued to accuse Oliver Cromwell's government of being far too aristocratic.

A pair of boots supposed to have belonged to Lilburne is on display at Sunderland Museum.

John Lingard (1771–1851)

Lingard was a Roman Catholic priest born in Winchester. In 1794, he was at Tudhoe with a few companions, then at Pontop Hall, and in 1795 took holy orders at Crook Hall, near Durham (now demolished). He taught natural and moral philosophy there and published letters in the *Newcastle Courant* in 1805, which were later published as *Catholic Loyalty Vindicated*. He also brought out *The Antiquities of the Anglo-Saxon Church* (1806, expanded 1845).

The establishment at Crook Hall was the forerunner of Ushaw College, where the students began to move in 1808, and where Southey visited Lingard. His later life, from 1811, was mostly spent at Hornby near Lancaster, where he wrote a *History of England* (1819–30). This idealised the Middle Ages and had considerable influence on writers like William Morris and the founders of the Oxford Movement.

John Thomas Looney (1870–1944)

Scholars of a certain type have always been irked that a towering genius like Shakespeare should have had such humble origins. Attempts have long been made to have Christopher Marlowe, or Francis Bacon, scholar and polymath, recognised as the true author of the plays. A scientist, on the other hand, might inquire why Bacon should pretend to be as scientifically ignorant as Shakespeare shows himself to be on a number of occasions.

John Thomas Looney, mercifully pronounced 'Loney,' is listed in Ward's Directory for 1899–1900 as a school teacher living at 119 Rodsley Avenue, Gateshead. He later resided at 15 Laburnum Gardens, Low Fell.

In 1920 he published, through Cecil Palmer in London, a monumental work whose short title is *Shakespeare Identified*. Here he suggests that the real author of Shakespeare's plays was Edmund de Vere, Earl of Oxford, who fitted Looney's deductions that Shakespeare was a nobleman of Lancastrian sympathies, with a fondness for Italy, a leaning towards Catholicism and a number of other distinguishing characteristics. Looney's book, which was researched in the Newcastle Lit and Phil, started a whole new avenue of speculation and has many followers today. Freud read it in 1923 and was at once converted. Even at the end of his life, in 1939, Freud repeats his view in the final revision of *An Outline of Psychoanalysis*.

Looney was a member of the Lit and Phil after 1911 and pays handsome tribute to the library, its unique system of operation, he says, ensured an ease and rapidity of work which would 'probably be impossible in any other institution in the country'. Looney presented the Lit and Phil with his edition of Edmund de Vere's poems in December 1927.

According to the *Gateshead Times* of 17 October 1948, Miss G. Looney, the youngest daughter of the Shakespearian scholar, was appointed head mistress of High West Street Infants.

James Losh (1763–1833)

On the staircase of the Lit and Phil building in Newcastle stands the imposing sculpted figure of James Losh, who lived at the Grove, Jesmond. Recorder of Newcastle and active in every progressive cause in the city and beyond, from the emancipation of the slaves to the Great Reform Bill of 1832, Losh was also a man of literature. He was a friend of Wordsworth and Coleridge, though he found Wordsworth's manner of conversation 'too earnest and emphatic'. He himself published an edition of Milton's *Areopagitica* (1791) and translated Benjamin Constant. Some of his own speeches were also published.

It seems he used to speak of having seen Marat at his father's house, Woodside, Wreay, near Carlisle, doubtless in the 1770s; a pleasant tradition has it that when walking the perilous Paris streets at the height of the Terror of 1792, the lordly Losh owed his survival to the protection of Marat.

Thomas Babington Macaulay (1800–1859)

Lord Macaulay was the uncle of George Otto Trevelyan of Wallington Hall, and the desk at which he wrote his famous *History of England* is in the study there. His much-anthologised 'A Jacobite's Epitaph', shows a fond familiarity with Teesdale:

> For him I languished in a foreign clime,
> Gray-haired with sorrow in my manhood's prime;
> Heard on Lavernia Scargill's whispering trees,
> And pined by Arno for my lovelier Tees . . .

Compton Mackenzie (1883–1972)

The Scottish man of letters, author of *Sinister Street* and *Whisky Galore*, is perhaps unique among writers in having spent long periods of his life on Herm in the Channel Islands and Barra in the Outer Hebrides (where he is buried). He was born about midway between the two, on 17 January 1883, at 23 Adelaide Street, West Hartlepool, in theatrical lodgings. His parents were appearing at the Gaiety Theatre.

Mackenzie was christened in Christ Church, West Hartlepool – the first major urban commission, incidentally, of the Victorian 'rogue' architect E. B. Lamb. Sir Nikolaus Pevsner remarks that the shape of the crossing-piers within 'defeats description'.

Baron Avro Manhattan (1914–1990)

Poet, artist and writer on religious, historical and allied themes, Manhattan spent much of his life after 1979 at the ornately decorated home of his wife's mother, 45 Henry Nelson Street, South Shields. The Baron, descended from the House of Savoy, was born in Italy to wealthy American/Dutch parents and was educated at the Sorbonne and the L.S.E.

Strikingly handsome in his youth, he was a member of the H. G. Wells set (and of the British Interplanetary Society), knew Bernard Shaw (whom he beat at bowls) and lived with Picasso for a while in Paris. He was also a close friend of Marie Stopes in the early 1950s.

By then, he had made a name with his book *The Vatican in World Politics* (1949), which ran to fifty editions. In all, he wrote some 60 books and published several during his South Shields period, including works on Vietnam and Ireland, the prophetic *Terror over Yugoslavia* in 1986 and *The Dawn of Man*, the fruit of 40 years of deliberation on evolutionary themes.

Both he and his wife loved South Shields, though they also had houses in Kensington and Spain. The Baron found the town an ideal place to work, and he often took refreshing walks along the pier and, in the summer, to Marsden. He enjoyed putting in the North Marine Park – and fish and chips and 'Broon Ale' as well!

Jean Paul Marat (1743–1793)

Marat was a medical man by profession and had worked on the continent and in London before coming in 1770 to Newcastle, where he practised for three years as a veterinary surgeon, though he is said to have accommodated humans also. He visited Newcastle again in 1775.

Though he had published scientific and philosophical tracts, his first overtly political work, *Chains of Slavery*, published in 1774 (in English), was probably written in Newcastle. By his own highly-coloured account, Marat had lived on black coffee and slept only two hours a night before completing the 65 chapters in three months – and had then slept for 13 days. Marat knew English well, though *Chains of Slavery* relies heavily on earlier works. The book purports to be: 'A work in which the clandestine and villainous attempts of Princes to ruin Liberty are pointed out, and the dreadful scenes of Despotism disclosed.' The French edition of 1792 was very similar in content, so one may say that the Marat who frequented the Newcastle patriotic clubs and Sand's circulating library in the Bigg Market, was the 'ami du peuple', the Marat of the Commune.

Christopher Marlowe (1564–1593)

Apart from Elizabeth I, who never ventured north of the Trent, most English rulers, from the Conqueror to Cromwell, have spent time in the North East, usually on serious business concerning Scotland. King John, Henry III, Edward I ('The Hammer of the Scots') and Edward III, all treated with the Scots at Alnwick and Newcastle. Being closer to the scene, Scottish kings have been in even greater evidence: two have been killed in the region, and two taken prisoner.

The queens of Edward I and II both preferred to stay at Tynemouth Castle when their husbands were campaigning in Scotland, and Christopher Marlowe's play, *Edward II*, is partly set there. The king indeed cries 'Welcome to Tynemouth!' – to the delight of local RSC audiences. Marlowe also mentions Killingworth. It was from Tynemouth that Edward II and his favourite, Piers Gaveston, fled by ship to Scarborough. The play is regarded as Marlowe's finest and was a significant influence on Shakespeare's *Richard II*.

Marlowe had violent, even criminal tendencies, and was, like Edward II, a murder victim, stabbed in a Deptford tavern after a quarrel over the bill. At the time, he was under warrant to appear before the Privy Council on unknown charges.

John Martin (1789–1854)

The scenery of Allendale was a major influence on the extraordinary painter, John Martin, who was born at Haydon Bridge. His great celestial landscape *The Plains of Heaven*, which is now in the Tate Gallery, is thought to be based on his native valley. Martin attended the grammar school in Haydon Bridge, until the family left for Newcastle, when the artist was 14 years old. He studied art there for some three years.

After moving to London, Martin began to paint the grandiose scenes of biblical destruction which are regarded as typical of his style. He is sometimes referred to as 'Mad' Martin, possibly through confusion with his brother Jonathan, who set fire to York Minster, or, more probably, his brother William, the 'poet and philosophical conjuror' as he called himself. William used to walk the streets of Newcastle in a hat made out of a tortoise-shell, mounted in brass. A designer of ingenious devices, he considered that the Stephensons had stolen his ideas for the safety lamp and the High Level Bridge. It must, however, be admitted that his poetry is at least on a par with that of William McGonagall. He spent his last years in his brother John's house in London.

John Martin achieved huge popularity: a print of his *Belshazzar's Feast*, adorned the Brontes' parlour wall at Haworth. Charlotte and Branwell copied his prints, and their juvenile stories, set in Angria and Glasstown, show the influence of Martin's fantasy architecture and landscape. Martin himself appears as Edward de Lisle of Verdopolis, painter of Babylon. Interestingly, one of the chief characters in the Angria stories is Alexander Percy, Earl of Northangerland. (We also recall that the heroine of *Shirley* has the surname Keeldar!)

Martin was greatly admired by the writers of the day; Charles Lamb writes of him with something approaching awe. Martin drew subjects from Lord Byron and Mary Shelley, and his spectacular painting of *The Bard* which now hangs in the Laing Art Gallery in Newcastle, is based on the poem by Thomas Gray. *The Last Man*, after the poet Thomas Campbell, is also in the gallery.

Martin, unsurprisingly, became a friend of the fantastic novelist, William Beckford, with whose grand and gloomy visions he felt a strong affinity. He also illustrated Milton's *Paradise Lost*, a subject eminently to his taste. His dramatic *Sadak in search of the Waters of Oblivion* may have inspired a passage in Keats' *Hyperion*, and Shelley certainly wrote a poem about it. Meanwhile, in France, Victor Hugo employed imagery taken from Martin, and French Romantic writers invented the word 'martinien' to describe the grandiose and spectacular.

Such extravagant popularity could hardly last. Martin was out of place in the age of Turner and Constable, neither of whom thought well of him. John Ruskin was also a severe critic. Nevertheless a large painting by Martin can fetch close to a million pounds today, and his influence can still be seen in the architecture and special effects of Hollywood biblical extravaganzas.

Harriet Martineau (1802–1876)

When the Grainger Market buildings in Newcastle were opened in 1835, the Green Market was incorporated and is mentioned by Harriet Martineau as a grandly-decorated place of evening promenade and dancing during the meeting of the British Association in Newcastle in 1838. Such was Harriet Martineau's celebrity that her sister borrowed an ear-trumpet and walked about the market, to draw away the throng from Harriet. She had arrived in the Tyne on a ship from Scotland with many of the participants, who good-naturedly shouted to the inquisitive folk of South Shields that they were 'savants', 'philosophers', 'nondescripts'!

Harriet Martineau contributed to Charles Dickens' magazine *Household Words* (he called her 'Hanny') and was a celebrated author in her own right at the time, having become a national figure with the huge success of her *Illustrations of Political Economy*. She was lionised in London society and wrote widely on many progressive subjects, like the enfranchisement of women and the establishment of a national system of education; she sometimes wrote several leaders a week for the *Daily News*.

Her chronic ill-health was a mystery to Victorian medicine, and she visited her brother-in-law, the celebrated Newcastle doctor Thomas Michael Greenhow, more than once to try to alleviate her symptoms – on the last occasion staying for six months in the family house at 28 Eldon Square. She then moved down-river to Tynemouth, where she stayed at Mrs Halliday's boarding house, 57 Front Street, for nearly five years from 16 March 1840. A plaque marks the house where she produced at least three books, including a novel about the Haitian slave leader, Toussaint L'Ouverture and *Life in the Sick-room*, describing her life in Tynemouth. She also devotes some hundred pages of her autobiography to this period.

She had expected to remain an invalid all her life, and delighted in the freedom her telescope allowed. Across the Tyne was the sandy beach, 'where there are frequent wrecks – too interesting to an invalid . . . and above the rocks, a spreading heath, where I watch troops of boys flying their kites; lovers and friends taking their breezy walk on Sundays . . .'

She gives a lyrical picture of Tynemouth:

When I look forth in the morning, the whole land may be sheeted with glittering snow, while the myrtle-green sea swells and tumbles . . . there is none of the deadness of winter in the landscape; no leafless trees, no locking up with ice; and the air comes in through my open upper sash, but sun-warmed. The robins twitter and hop in my flower-boxes . . . and at night, what a heaven! What an expanse of stars above, appearing more steadfast, the more the Northern Lights dart and quiver!

Eventually, in 1844, following Spencer Timothy Hall's performances in Newcastle, she was successfully treated by mesmerism. Her natural enthusiasm for the controversial method caused friction with her family and led to her leaving Tynemouth and moving to Ambleside where she died in 1876.

The busybody Mrs Jellyby, in *Bleak House*, with her aim of getting women into parliament, is based on Harriet Martineau. Dickens came to regard her as wrong-headed, vain and a humbug, but she retained her high regard for Dickens.

Gavin Maxwell (1914–1969)

Despite his impressive works on Iraq, Sicily and Morocco, Maxwell is best known for his splendid otter books, in particular *Ring of Bright*

Water. Maxwell was the son of the beautiful Lady Mary Percy, daughter of the seventh Duke of Northumberland, and spent time as a boy at Alnwick Castle. He recalled a sense of constriction there, not surprisingly for a future soldier and adventurer.

Maxwell was deeply influenced by the South Shields-born naturalist and writer, Ernest Thompson Seton, all of whose books he had read by the time he was eight years old. *Wild Animals I have Known* was probably his favourite.

The title *Ring of Bright Water* is actually taken from a hauntingly beautiful poem by the poet Kathleen Raine, though it should be emphasised that the poem does not refer to Maxwell. The tortuous relationship between Raine and Maxwell is treated in *The Lion's Mouth*, the third volume of her autobiography. Though born in Essex, Kathleen Raine was of northern stock. Her parents had met at Armstrong College in Newcastle and her grandfather taught in Kielder. As a child during World War I she spent some two years at the manse in Great Bavington with her Aunt Peggy, and ever afterwards recalled Northumberland as Eden.

James Melville (1556–1614)
The Scottish poet and diarist was a staunch Presbyterian, and his opposition to bishops in his native land caused him to flee to Berwick in May 1584, to escape the attacks of his enemy Bishop Adamson. While there, he spent some time in Newcastle. Back in Scotland after 1585, Melville was again in the forefront of controversy.

He was summoned to London in 1606, with his uncle, Andrew Melville, to discuss church policy with James I. As a result of these talks, Andrew Melville ended in the Tower, where he lingered for four years. James, however, was ordered to remain in Newcastle and not stray more than ten miles from it. He stayed there for seven years, during which time he was promised rewards if he supported the royal plans – even being conducted as far as Berwick to persuade him. He was adamant, and refused a move to Carlisle also. In 1613, negotiations started for his return to Scotland, but he died in Berwick in January 1614.

His poetry, some of it written in his Newcastle exile, is rather deficient technically and lacks originality. It certainly compares unfavourably with his talented uncle's output. *The Diary of Mr James Melville 1556–1601*, however, is a fresh and lively portrait of his times. It is very direct in describing his contemporaries – his sketch of John Knox at St Andrews is particularly effective.

Henry Seton Merriman (1862–1903)
Merriman was the pseudonym of Hugh Stowell Scott, who was born in Newcastle, at 16 Rye Hill. He abandoned a career at Lloyd's, to travel and write a series of stirring novels, often with foreign settings – perhaps the most famous being the Napoleonic *Barlasch of the Guard* (1903). He did not forget his roots however. In July 1901, he published a story in *Northern Counties Magazine*, which features a Tyne-built ship, the *Giralda*, some Geordie speech and 'the prettiest girl in South Shields'. Merriman's great popularity is shown by the publication of a memorial edition of his works in 1909–10, comprising fourteen volumes.

Wilfrid Meynell (1852–1948)

At the far end of Ellison Place in Newcastle once stood Picton Place, now demolished to make way for the motorway. Here, at Picton House, Wilfrid Meynell (then written Mennell) was born. A Catholic convert at 18, Wilfrid went on to become a considerable man of letters, editing Catholic journals and producing articles, poems and stories, as well as a practical handbook, *Journals and Journalism*, in 1880.

Nowadays, his wife Alice has the greater reputation as both essayist and poet. The couple collaborated on the periodical *Merry England* for twelve years and on many other literary projects during their forty-five years of marriage, during which their home was a centre of Roman Catholic activity. Their son, Sir Francis Meynell, founded the famous Nonesuch Press.

Wilfrid's greatest service to literature is no doubt his discovery and rescue of Francis Thompson, who remained as an adopted son in the Meynell household for nineteen years. Thompson, who had studied for the Catholic priesthood at Ushaw College near Durham, was by now an opium addict and living in extreme poverty in London, reduced to selling matches. He sent some poems in to *Merry England*, and from then on the Meynells looked after him till his death from tuberculosis in 1907. 'The Hound of Heaven', referring to the pursuit of the soul by God, is one of the most anthologised poems in the language.

Elizabeth Montagu (1720–1800)

'The queen of literary London' for fifty years in the eighteenth century, Elizabeth Montagu was a frequent visitor to the family manor house at East Denton Hall, a clean-lined mansion of 1622 along the West Road in Newcastle. She was much admired for her *Essay on Shakespeare* of 1769, and her London salon was graced by the leading men of the day. Doctor Johnson praised her conversation and called her 'Queen of the Blues'. Sir Benjamin Stillingfleet was wont to attend her soirees wearing his blue worsted stockings, instead of the usual black silk – causing the epithet 'bluestocking', which had historic antecedents in Venice and Paris, to be applied in England to any woman of intellectual pretensions.

Elizabeth visited Denton and the Montagu collieries frequently between 1758 and 1789, though on her first trip she was inclined to share her London friends' fears that Newcastle was within the Arctic Circle, and brought food just in case! At all events, Lady Elizabeth was soon quite at home in Newcastle, enjoying an energetic social life and ordering Northumbrian delicacies for her houses in London and Berkshire. She was a shrewd businesswoman, despite affecting to patronise Northumbrian society for its practical conversation. Though acting as Lady Bountiful to her miners and their families, she was pleased at how cheap this could be. She was also glad to note that: 'Our pitmen are afraid of being turned off and that fear keeps an order and regularity amongst them that is very uncommon.' Elizabeth certainly considered their dialect 'dreadful to the auditor's nerves'. Charleton's *Newcastle Town* says that she was 'as beautiful as he was clever and as good as she was beautiful'. What her miners thought of her, however, is not recorded.

William Morris (1834–1896)

The celebrated poet, craftsman and socialist was the author of *News from Nowhere* (1890), the influential vision of a pastoral utopia, as well as much mediaevalist verse like *The Earthly Pardise*.

He had founded Morris and Co. in 1861 with Pre-Raphaelite artist friends, including Rossetti, and there is much of interest by the firm in the North East. There is a splendid display in the church at Brampton; Christ Church, Sunderland also has a fine East window, while E. S. Prior's grand church of 1906–7, St Andrew, Roker, probably the best in the country of its date, contains tapestry and carpeting by Morris and Co.

It was at Bensham Grove in Gateshead, which also has Morris and Co. stained glass, tiles and fittings, that Robert Spence Watson entertained William Morris, who was visiting the North East in the late 1880s. There was much debate in the house with local politicians and churchmen on society and democracy. Spence Watson describes Morris as 'so attractive, so fiery, so unpractical'. Morris would declaim: 'It's a revolution we must have, a bloody revolution if need be.' Priestley visited Bensham Grove in 1933 in the course of his *English Journey* but was not aware of this relevant piece of history.

On Easter Monday, 11 April 1887, Morris, after a six mile march to Hartford near Blyth, addressed a meeting of miners while perched on a plank, in response to the cry: 'If yon man does na stand on the top, we canna hear him!' Morris found it very inspiring to speak to such a big crowd of eager and serious persons: 'I did pretty well and didn't stumble at all.' After a train journey to Newcastle, where Morris met Joseph Cowen in the refreshment room ('very friendly and nice, I must say'), the company went on to Ryton Willows along the Tyne for another successful meeting, among the swings, cricket and dancing.

Robert Morrison (1782–1834)

Morrison was born at Buller's Green, Morpeth, though the family moved to Newcastle when he was three. In 1798, he joined the Presbyterian church and attended the High Bridge Meeting-House in the city. He eventually became the first Protestant missionary to China.

He was appointed translator to the East India Company on 20 February 1809. In 1815, the directors learned that Morrison had published the New Testament in Chinese and, like all other authorities in history faced with the prospect of a vernacular bible, were alarmed. They felt that it might turn the Chinese against the company, and considered dismissing Morrison. He retained his position, however, and remained active in the missionary field.

Morrison was a voluminous writer in both English and Chinese, his great work in Chinese being his translation of the bible (1814–19). His *Dictionary of the Chinese Language* (1815–23) was published at Malacca in 21 volumes.

John Bingham Morton (1893–1979)

Writing as 'Beachcomber', Morton brought delight to readers of the *Daily Express* for fifty years with his surreal humour. He was also a great walker, and one trip took him across the Cheviots. He visited

Hexham, where he notes that the women all walked sideways, and obliges us with a verse or two about the deficiencies of the Roman Wall in keeping the Scots at bay.

Morton appears to have headed towards Jedburgh by way of the North Tyne valley, eventually crossing the Deadwater Burn. He has poetic fun with all the strange names in the region, but climbing was hard and his tribute is heartfelt:

> As soon as you get to the top of a rise, you have to plunge down to cross some tiresome but very beautiful burn. The air is full of the sound of running water.
> I have never been in such a lovely spot in England.

Thomas Morton (?1764–1838)

Morton was born in County Durham. Sent to Lincoln's Inn in London, he preferred cricket to the law and became a senior member of the MCC.

He scored an influential success with a musical *The Children in the Wood* (1793) and was the author of several successful comedies written for the Covent Garden Theatre, including *Speed the Plough* (1798). This introduced the (invisible) character of Mrs Grundy as the voice of conventional morality.

Morton's son, John (1811–1891) wrote the famous farce *Box and Cox* in 1847.

James Murray (1732–1782)

The author of *Sermons to Asses* (1768) studied in Edinburgh, was minister in Alnwick in 1761 and by 1764 was minister of the High Bridge Meeting-House in Newcastle.

Murray wrote a little book called *The Travels of the Imagination: a True Journey from Newcastle to London* in 1772, which gives an interesting glimpse of the Tyne ferry, which plied between the Swirle, in Sandgate, and the southern bank while the bridge was being repaired.

Charleton refers to Murray as a worthy son of the Covenanters, a notable man in his day and a voluminous writer. He wrote *A History of the Churches of England and Scotland* and *A History of the American War* (1778). He was an outspoken man and frequently in trouble. He seems at the time of his London trip to have been in some danger of arrest, having just preached from the text: 'He that hath not a sword, let him sell his garments and buy one.' Of the ferry, Murray remarks that it took a year to cross. Of the ferryman, he says: 'You wait the pleasure of a little arbitrary *bashaw*, who will not move one foot beyond the rules of his own authority, or mitigate the sentences passed upon those who are condemned to travel in a stage-coach within a ferry-boat.'

Nikolai Ogaryov (1813–1877)

The unpretentious building at 66 Westmorland Road in Newcastle, is where Nikolai Ogaryov lived for a few months in 1874. His name is known to every Russian, not only as a poet, but as the fellow-exile and collaborator of the great Alexander Herzen on the newspaper *The Bell*, which was printed in England and smuggled into Russia.

The oath the two young men swore on the Sparrow hills above Moscow in 1840, not to rest until their country was set free, is again something all Russians know. It sustained them and their friends throughout the many crises of their lives at home and abroad, memorably described in E. H. Carr's *The Romantic Exiles*.

In October 1874, Ogaryov was living in Hawthorn Terrace (or possibly Hawthorn Place), at the house of 'my friend' Charles Wood, a local businessman. In November, he was at the house of a Mrs Smith at 66, Westmorland Road. How Ogaryov spent his time in the city has still to be researched, though he was very pleased to have arrived in Newcastle – as well he might be after a sea journey with his beloved Mary (and his furniture) all the way from Genoa. While in Newcastle, Ogaryov worked on his 'Confession in Verse' and his 'Last Curse' (unfinished), which is about his materialist conception of history.

The end of the year, however, saw the couple in Mary's home town of Greenwich, where Ogaryov died in 1877, still active in the cause of freedom.

Anne Ogle (1832–1918)

Anne Ogle was born at the vicarage in Bedlington. This is now a service wing to the present vicarage of 1835.

She was a shy and retiring girl and lived most of her life in Northumberland, eventually moving to her sister's house at Chesters on the Roman Wall, near Hexham. Her first novel *A Lost Love* (1854), published as by 'Ashford Owen' is in part autobiographical, reflecting her own restricted youth; the heroine is called Georgy Sandon in homage to George Sand. It had considerable success and led to her becoming acquainted with the Brownings, Tennyson and Thackeray. Her only other published novel *The Story of Catherine* (1885), like the first, depicts the conventional restriction of woman's freedom of action.

Augustus Hare visited Chesters on 6 October 1896, 'with the widow and children of my dear old friend George Clayton and Miss Annie Ogle, whom I knew so well in those far-off days, here as a delightful *old* lady, with snow-white hair, but the same winning character and ways as in her youth.'

Margaret Oliphant (1828–1897)

William Bell Scott's Edinburgh friend, the designer Francis Oliphant, worked for William Wailes' thriving Newcastle stained-glass concern, and in 1844 showed Scott a poem written by his precocious young cousin, Margaret Wilson. Oliphant eventually married her in Liverpool in 1852.

By this time Margaret, who thus became the celebrated Mrs Oliphant, had already published two novels. According to Charleton's *History of Newcastle Town*, the Oliphants resided in the town for some time before going to London in 1853, where Mrs Oliphant wrote some 100 novels as well as short stories and great numbers of articles for magazines. Scott was not impressed, however, and grumpily calls her facility: 'An instance of experiments in popular invention and in making bricks without straw truly wonderful.'

George Orwell (1903–1950)

Orwell met the Tyneside writer Jack Common in 1930, when the latter was working for the *Adelphi* magazine in London. The two became friends, and in the 1930s lived about ten miles apart in Hertfordshire. They corresponded and paid visits to one another; when Orwell was abroad in 1938–39, Common lived in his cottage at Wallington. As a genuine proletarian, Common was able to regard Orwell without sentimentality, and his comments are typically provocative and intriguing: 'My friendship with Eric began in disappointment and grew under mutual suspicion.'

Eileen (O'Shaughnessy), Orwell's wife, died on 29 March 1945 at Fernwood House, in Clayton Road, Jesmond, in Newcastle, the former home of old Sir Walter Runciman the shipowner. The house was by then a private clinic and she had been undergoing an operation. The letter she was writing when she was taken away to be operated on was left poignantly half-finished.

Eileen O'Shaughnessy was born in South Shields on 25 September 1905, and educated at Sunderland High School and Oxford. She and Orwell had married in 1936 and Orwell writes affectionately of her and her unflagging support from the Spanish Civil War onwards. She appears as Rosemary Waterlow in his novel *Keep the Aspidistra Flying*. During the war, she worked with the novelist Lettice Cooper at the Ministry of Food, preparing recipes and scripts for 'The Kitchen Front', a regular morning broadcast. The character of Ann in Lettice Cooper's 1947 novel, *Black Bethlehem* is clearly based on Eileen. Professor Bernard Crick, in his great biography of Orwell, remarks that many features of the Ministry of Truth in *Nineteen Eighty-Four* owed as much to her experiences in the Ministry of Food as to Orwell's at the BBC.

Orwell had been on the continent as a war correspondent when he heard of his wife's death. He hurried back to England and by 1 April, he was at Greystones, in Carlton, near Stockton, where Eileen, together with the Orwells' adopted son, Richard, had been staying prior to the operation. The house belonged to her sister-in-law, Gwen, a doctor who had found Richard for them among the unwanted wartime babies she encountered in her practice. She had also arranged the fateful operation in Newcastle.

Eileen's body was taken for burial from 20 Haldane Terrace and the funeral took place on 3 April 1945 in St Andrew's cemetery, Jesmond. The grave, which lies near the cemetery lodge, close to the left hand chapel, has a headstone, paid for by Eric Arthur Blair (Orwell himself). It is inscribed 'Eileen Blair (nee O'Shaughnessy)', and is located in section B, number 145. Orwell revisited the grave on his way to Scotland early in May 1946.

Mary Oxley (fl. 1650)

Mary Oxley was a Scots poet living in Morpeth. She wrote an 'Encomium' on her friend, the famous Scottish poet William Drummond of Hawthornden, who had died in 1649. This was published, along with his poems, in an edition of 1656 by Thomas Phillips, John Milton's nephew. She added a preface to her poem, in which she suggests that 'hoarse encumbrances of household care' prevented her being a better poet.

Phillips, in 1675, mentions her 'many other things in Poetry', but these are not known.

Cyril Northcote Parkinson (1909–1993)

Parkinson was the son of the art master at Barnard Castle School and was born at 45 Galgate (now council offices) in that town on 30 July 1909. Though in later life he became Raffles Professor of History in Singapore, as well as being an artist and journalist, he is best known for the 'law' that bears his name, formulated in the book *Parkinson's Law*. The basic law, which has now become part of the language, states that work expands to fill the time available for its completion.

Other applications demonstrate how bureaucrats spawn deputies; how naval administrators multiply as the number of ships declines, and how one can tell that an organisation is in terminal decline when it inhabits a vast polished palace. Firms which are really vigorous live up uncarpeted staircases in rooms full of boxes. Other witty and literate books like *In-Laws and Outlaws*, *Left Luggage* and *East and West* – described as: 'A lively intellect ranges over the whole history of mankind' – kept him in the news.

Though Parkinson became a household name, he was patronised with adjectives like 'irreverent' and 'provocative' and eventually suffered the usual fate of those who do not care to be solemn; he was not taken seriously.

Thomas Percy (1729–1811)

The influence of the great Border ballads of the region runs like a thread through the present compilation, from Ben Jonson to Basil Bunting. It was Thomas Percy, a man of wide intellectual and antiquarian interests, who really brought ballad poetry, particularly the Border ballads, to the attention of the literary world in his *Reliques of Ancient English Poetry* (1765) and so helped to pave the way for the Romantic movement. Percy, incidentally, states that most of the minstrels who sang the ballads in the fifteenth and sixteenth centuries belonged to the north. These were the performers that Elizabethans like Sir Philip Sidney would have heard.

The activities of Sir Walter Scott and others in the nineteenth century gave the ballads an even wider popularity. William Morris considered them to be the greatest poems in the language, while Swinburne knew virtually all of them by heart. Percy's *Reliques* achieved considerable popularity, going through four editions by 1794, though it also attracted the hostility of such as Joseph Ritson for its unscholarly approach. The Newcastle Society of Antiquaries published the pioneering *Northumbrian Minstrelsy* in 1882.

A ballad fragment survives of a thirteenth century affray between the Prior of Durham and Lord Neville of Raby, when the nobleman's retainers were beaten off with candelsticks. This points to a lost ballad tradition much earlier than the one we possess.

It was at Barras Bridge in 1388 that Henry Percy, known as Hotspur for his reckless courage, clashed in single combat with the Scottish chieftain James, Earl of Douglas, under the walls of Newcastle. This skirmish was a prelude to the Battle of Otterburn, fought by moonlight on 15 August 1388, when Douglas was killed and Hotspur captured. Jean Froissart, who visited England and

Scotland in 1356, 1361 and again in 1394–95, calls it in his celebrated *Chronicles* of the Hundred Years War, 'the best-fought and severest of all battles'. This encounter is described in The Battle of Otterbourne, which is included in Thomas Percy's *Reliques*:

> And they hae burnt the dales o' Tyne
> And part of Bamburghshire,
> And three good towers on Redeswire fells
> They left them all on fire.

This ballad is often confused with another, the stirring *Chevy Chase* (not included by Percy), which tells of the Earl of Northumberland's vow to hunt for three days across the Scottish border. It ends with the death of both Earl Percy and Douglas. Of it, the Elizabethan courtier, soldier and poet, Sir Philip Sidney famously said: 'I never heard the old song of Percy and Douglas that I found not my heart moved more than with a trumpet.' Ben Jonson went so far as to remark that he would give all his works to have written *Chevy Chase*.

The sombre atmosphere of the ballads mirrors a harsh, often ruthless society, and harks back to the heroic Anglo-Saxon poems where courage and fortitude are the prime virtues: happiness and kindness are rare, and religion absent. Nevertheless, few even today can resist the stirring of the blood that Sidney felt.

Froissart, incidentally, the most vivid and readable of the mediaeval chroniclers, can be over-imaginative. He says that he rode the entire length of the Roman Wall in 1361, on his way back from Scotland. On reaching Carlisle, he rejoiced to think that he was in Carlyon, King Arthur's capital.

After becoming chaplain to the Duke of Northumberland, Thomas Percy began to imagine that he himself belonged to the great family. He wrote a ballad *The Hermit of Warkworth* (1771), in which the name Marmion first appears, and later quarrelled with Samuel Johnson over Thomas Pennant's descriptions of Northumberland and Alnwick Castle. When Johnson said that he too had passed through Alnwick, Percy remarked: 'But my good friend, you are short-sighted, and do not see so well as I do.' Johnson forgave him, saying he was a man 'out of whose company I never go without having learned something'.

Anna Maria Porter (1780–1832)

Anna Porter, poet, novelist and sister of Jane, was born in Durham, the youngest child of an army surgeon who died before her birth. She was in London by the 1790s, publishing verse in the *Universal Magazine*. After her *Artless Tales*, she also wrote a short novel, *Walsh Colville* published anonymously in 1797. Though her sister was the more popular writer, Anna was the more prolific. *The Hungarian Brothers* (1807), a stirring historical romance set against the French Revolutionary war was a considerable success and went into several editions. She also produced the humanitarian *Tales of Pity on Fishing, Shooting and Hunting* in 1814 and collaborated with her sister in collections of stories.

In all, she published some thirty works, many being published in the USA and translated into French. She died of typhus, aged 42.

Jane Porter (1776–1850)

Anna's sister, Jane Porter, seems also to have been born in Durham. After her father's death, the family moved to Edinburgh, where Walter Scott, a frequent visitor, regaled the girls with tales of times gone by. Jane's novel *Thaddeus of Warsaw* (1803) is one of the earliest examples of the historical novel, and went through a dozen editions; it was based on eye-witness accounts from Polish refugees of the doomed independence struggle of the 1790s. *The Scottish Chiefs* (1810), a novel about William Wallace, was also a success (the French version was banned by Napoleon) and has remained popular with Scottish children. Her method of uniting history with imaginative writing was taken up by Walter Scott himself in 1814.

Jane and Anna, who later lived in London and Surrey, were sisters of Sir Robert Ker Porter, the artist, with whom Jane often worked in co-operation.

John Boynton Priestley (1894–1984)

At the behest of his publisher, Priestley made a tour of the depressed areas of England in late 1933. Published as *English Journey*, the book addresses a metropolitan audience and has been oddly influential in establishing the 'image' of the North East, even locally, for over sixty years.

Priestley, originally a headmaster's son from Bradford, was by now an established London writer and journalist. Though he had been stationed in Tynemouth as a young soldier in late 1915, and had enjoyed Newcastle theatres and music halls, Priestley admits that he had taken a dislike to the whole area.

Some twenty years later, he records his surprise at the fine buildings (none named), according Newcastle 'a certain sombre dignity'. By contrast with other cities on his itinerary, however, Priestley is utterly ignorant of Newcastle history. The Emperor Hadrian is only mentioned in connection with York, even though Priestley stood on the course of Hadrian's Wall in Newcastle. Even its theatres – Priestley was a successful dramatist after all – make no appearance, though in other cities they are prominent.

Nor do there seem to be any warm interiors in which to be cosily civilised (a favourite word) with local antiquarians, as he had found elsewhere. The book in fact completely ignores the lighter side of Tyneside life, concentrating solely on the human cost of recession in the basic North East industries and, above all, the intense aesthetic anguish Priestley felt at the ugliness of the contemporary urban industrial scene. Priestley always hankered after a pre-industrial 'green' England and seems to have thought Newcastle was a product of the nineteenth century, a town built for work. Now the work had gone, the place had no purpose.

Priestley came to Newcastle, where he knew almost nobody, on a wet November night. This sets the tone for his approach. Like any outside observer, he comments vaguely, though not unsympathetically, on hotels, transport, food, and whatever quirks and local habits happen to strike his eye and ear. Like Dickens and Ivor Gurney, he found the locals uncouth, even compared to his native Bradford (though not so bad when you got to know them), and considered the local speech barbarous, monotonous and irritating, whether spoken by men or women.

Again by contrast with other places, he distances Tyneside unsympathetically from the reader by naming virtually no streets or locations, apart from Jesmond Dene, and St James' Hall, where he describes the boxing (with some appropriately repellent, bludgeoning prose). The effect is monotonous and alienating. Though he crossed the Tyne Bridge and was impressed by Robert Stephenson's High Level Bridge, he names neither.

Close by, stands the Bridge Hotel (unnamed), where Priestley was astonished to see the Peoples' Theatre rehearsing Euripides' *Trojan Women*, and has left us a patronising account.

With some exceptions, like South Shields, Priestley took a very scathing view of 1930s Tyneside (particularly Gateshead) as a place for human beings to live. His impressions are superficial, however, and there is none of the analysis of everyday economics that we find in Orwell's northern trip. By contrast with his knowledgeable remarks in York and Lincoln, for example, he knows nothing of the Tyneside Jewish community, and is also amazed to see a synagogue in Sunderland. He admits that worsening weather played a large part in shaping his emotions and he suffered from a throbbing head cold throughout his stay. He advises the reader to take this into account. Very few do.

Priestley's humanity and pity are therefore declaimed (often with powerful rhetoric) rather than conveyed, and are so overdone in the Durham coalfield (the only mining area he visited on his journey) that he actually makes things appear worse than they were. Shotton sounds like something out of Dante's *Inferno*. Once again, informed by a German lady that the Durham village children are actually more musical than their continental counterparts, he simply cannot believe his ears. Priestley must be the only writer ever to mention Durham Castle (twice) but not the Cathedral – and certainly the only one ever to advise tourists not to go to the city!

Sir Thomas Wemyss Reid (1842–1905)

Reid was born and brought up in Newcastle, where he became chief reporter on the *Newcastle Journal* at the age of 19. While on the *Leeds Mercury* (1870–87), he obtained the right of provincial newspaper reporters to be admitted to the House of Commons press gallery.

In 1887, he became the manager of Cassells the publishers in London, and was knighted in 1894. From 1890–1899, Reid edited his own moderate Liberal magazine, *The Speaker* and wrote a number of biographies, including one of Charlotte Bronte. He also wrote a book on Tunis, *Land of the Bey* (1882) and a number of popular novels like *Gladys Fane* (1883).

Richard and John of Hexham (fl 1129–54)

Richard, Prior of Hexham, was a Northumbrian chronicler, who continued the work of Simeon of Durham from 1129. Richard's son John, also Prior of Hexham, continued the chronicle until the end of King Stephen's reign in 1154. Both chroniclers are highly valued for the amount of original material they offer about a very turbulent period of English history, including the Battle of the Standard, near Northallerton, in 1138.

Nicholas Ridley (c 1500–1555)

A scion of the famous Northumberland family, the celebrated Protestant martyr was born at either Williemoteswick, near Haydon Bridge, or Unthank Hall near Haltwhistle. According to his brother, 'he learned his grammar with great dexterity in Newcastle'.

At Cambridge, Ridley gradually came to reject many Roman Catholic doctrines. When he eventually became Bishop of London he promoted reformed opinions, while being distinguished for learning, generosity and firmness of principle. He assisted Archbishop Cranmer in the preparation of the Thirty Nine Articles and his influence is also thought to be detectable in the two revisions of the prayer-book by Edward VI.

On the king's death, Ridley publicly denounced the Tudor princesses, Mary and Elizabeth, as illegitimate, and espoused the cause of Lady Jane Grey, the Earl of Northumberland's protégée, as a Protestant queen. He was sent to the Tower by Mary in June 1553 and eventually tried as a heretic at Oxford. He refused to recant and was burnt at the stake there on 16 October 1555. His last letter was written to his 'dear Cousin', John Ridley of the Walltown', referring to the farm on the slope south of the Roman Wall, near his birthplace.

Thomas Latimer, who suffered with him, spoke words which have entered the language: 'Be of good comfort, Master Ridley, and play the man. We shall this day light a candle, by God's grace, in England, as I trust shall never be put out.' The Martyrs memorial in Oxford marks the spot where the two died.

Apart from his work on the prayer-book, Ridley wrote a good deal, though much has been lost. He published little in his lifetime, but several theological treatises appeared after his death. *The Works of Nicholas Ridley* were published in 1841.

Joseph Ritson (1752–1803)

Ritson was born in the High Street, Stockton and spent most of his youth in a house in Silver Street. He went to London in 1775 and practised as a conveyancer, but devoted most of his time to antiquarian studies, publishing 36 volumes during the last twenty years of his life (ten more came out after his death).

Given to furious and insulting (though usually justified) attacks on the work of fellow scholars, such as Warton, Thomas Percy and Doctor Johnson, he seems to have retained the friendship of Robert Surtees and Sir Walter Scott, who consulted him while working on his *Border Minstrelsy*. William Godwin was an intimate in London, and Ritson assisted him with historical background for his great novel *Caleb Williams*. Robert Burns once said that it was a collection of old ballads edited by Ritson that he read every day as he tramped to his work at the plough.

At the theatre in Green-Dragon Yard in Stockton, Ritson had encountered Thomas Holcroft, the novelist and radical and one of the most remarkable men of his time, then making a living as a strolling player. Holcroft too became an intimate friend of Godwin and Ritson. An encounter with Hutchinson, the poet, prompted Ritson to attempt verse himself (he was eccentric in spelling also):

> Where Tease in sweet meanders slowly glides,
> And, gently murm'ring rolls his easy tides,
> There stands a town, with peace and plenty crown'd;
> Far-famed for dames, wise, charitable, chaste,
> And first in beauty's annals ever plac'd.
> In every age has STOCKTON been rever'd,
> Her sons have always been belov'd and fear'd.

Ritson's book on Robin Hood came out in 1795, with illustrations by Thomas Bewick; he also published several collections of songs, fairy tales and verses for children. 'Taffy was a Welshman' and 'Ride a Cockhorse' are only two among those included in the booklet printed by R. Christopher, the Stockton publisher.

Ritson's irascible temperament was made worse by ill-health. His diet, originally inspired by reading Mandeville's *Fable of the Bees*, became increasingly vegetarian. He lived on vegetables, biscuits, tea and lemonade, and eventually had to sell half his library to survive. He finally went insane in September 1803, barricaded himself in and made a bonfire of manuscripts. He died later that month.

Michael Roberts (1902–1948)

Poet, critic and editor, Roberts taught at the Royal Grammar School in Newcastle for sixteen years after 1925, apart from an interval in the early 30s in London. Oddly enough, one of the fellow-boarders in his Jesmond guest-house in 1925 was Captain W. E. Johns. Later, Roberts lived at Red Lodge in Longbenton, now gone, where he papered a wall up to the ceiling with rejection slips.

Subsequently, his anthologies *New Signatures* (1932) and *New Country* (1933), containing work by William Empson, Auden, Spender, Day-Lewis and others, had made him, in T. S. Eliot's phrase, 'expositor and interpreter of the poetry of his generation.' Roberts edited the influential *Faber Book of Modern Verse* (1936).

In 1935 Roberts married Janet Adam Smith, also a gifted writer and anthologist. She was the editor of *The Faber Book of Childrens' Verse* (still in print) and had been assistant editor of *The Listener* in 1933, when she incurred the wrath of the formidable Lord Reith, the BBC Director General, by having Auden's poem 'The Witnesses' printed in the magazine's poetry supplement. Lord Reith found it incomprehensible.

The couple lived at 13 Fern Avenue, Jesmond, from June 1935 to April 1939, then at no. 73 for the birth of their second child (and still later at 49A Wordsworth Street in Penrith, 1939–41, when the RGS was evacuated). Janet Adam Smith writes of those Newcastle years as 'a tale of poems, children, books, anthologies, reviews, climbing, ski-ing, school camps and holidays in Lakes, Highlands and Alps.'

Auden had written to Roberts in 1932 for advice on his teaching career and, later, about his play *The Ascent of F6*. On 27 September, 1937 he came to dinner at 13 Fern Avenue, Jesmond, when the couple's first baby was three weeks old. Always fascinated by medical matters, he talked much with the midwife in attendance, Nurse

Laverick, and elicited a fund of stories drawn from her Newcastle experience.

Michael Roberts' own poetry is often about the mountains where he and his wife were very much at home, but 'HMS Hero' and 'Temperance Festival: Town Moor, Newcastle' have local interest – and 'Hymn to the Sun' begins:

> 'Voy wawm' said the dustman
> one bright August morning –
> but that was in Longbenton,
> under the trees.

Dante Gabriel Rossetti (1828–1882)

Rossetti, an important and influential figure in Victorian literature, had founded the Pre-Raphaelite Brotherhood in 1848, intending to bring about a revolution in poetry and painting. His own poetry had strong Arthurian and ballad leanings, though overburdened with cloudy generalisations on life and death. Rossetti's translations and letters are also of interest.

He spent several weeks with William Bell Scott at 14 St Thomas Crescent, Newcastle in 1853. According to Scott's *Autobiographical Notes* (1892):

> D. G. Rossetti made a visit of some weeks to me at Newcastle in 1853, when I was preparing my little volume, sometimes called *Poems by a Painter*, from a frontispiece so inscribed. He brought with him some of his own poetry in manuscript, sonnets and other works, so we had much talk of poetry in the first place and of friends in the second, which last subject in his mouth was amusing enough . . . This visit to Newcastle was partly a holiday for his health. When he left, still complaining, I took him to Hexham . . . and on to Carlisle and Wetheral, where we parted.

In fact, Rossetti had disliked Newcastle and was only happy when he reached the countryside. He particularly liked Hexham, where the two friends sat surveying the busy market scene through the window of an inn.

The studio at 14 St Thomas Crescent in Newcastle, where Rossetti painted the portrait of Maria Leathart in December 1862, still stands at the rear of the house.

John Rushworth (c 1612–1690)

'Historical John', as Thomas Carlyle called him, was born at Acklington Park, Warkworth. His great claim to fame lies in the *Historical Collections* (8 volumes published 1659–1701), compiled from shorthand notes taken down at actual meetings of the Star Chamber, Exchequer Chamber and Parliament, covering the period down to 1648. He was appointed assistant clerk to the Long Parliament in 1640 and was on duty on 4 January 1642, when King Charles I came to arrest the five members; he made notes of the king's speech, which the king ordered to be published. Rushworth similarly recorded the trial of Strafford.

He was often employed as messenger between king and parliament and was appointed secretary to Sir Thomas Fairfax (1645–48). He wrote an eye-witness account of the battle of Naseby, and was later secretary to Cromwell for a short time. Rushworth sat several times as parliamentary representative for Berwick and was also a freeman of Newcastle upon Tyne.

The *Historical Collections* are regarded as the most valuable source available for the study of the Civil War period and it is a curious fact that during the constitutional arguments that raged between the American colonists and the British government in the period leading up to the American War of Independence, Rushworth played a posthumous role. 'What we did,' said Jefferson, 'was with the help of Rushworth, whom we rummaged over for revolutionary precedents of those days.'

According to the Harleian MS. 7524 (says Isaac D'Israeli in his *Curiosities of Literature*), Rushworth passed the last years of his life in jail, where he died. After the Restoration, when he presented to the king several of the Privy Council's books, which he had preserved from ruin, he received for his only reward the *thanks of his majesty*.

John Ruskin (1819–1900)

The great art critic and social thinker was at Wallington Hall in 1853, with his wife Effie and the Pre-Raphaelite painter Millais. It was from there that the trio set out on their fateful journey to Glenfinlas in the Trossachs, where Millais painted his celebrated portrait of Ruskin against a background of striking scenery. The Ruskins' marriage was an unhappy one, and had not been consummated. Millais fell in love with Effie on this trip and few portraits can have been executed in such strained circumstances. Though the divorce proceedings were protracted and scandalous, the marriage was at length annulled and Millais and Effie were married in 1855. On the whole, it was felt that Ruskin was to blame, but Queen Victoria refused to receive Effie until Millais requested it as a favour on his deathbed.

Lady Pauline Trevelyan had met Ruskin through her own literary activities – she wrote reviews for the *Edinburgh Review* and *The Scotsman* – and introduced him to William Bell Scott, but this was not a success. Bell Scott was painting the new covered hall at Wallington with scenes from North East history, and Ruskin and the other guests set about decorating the pillars with flower paintings. Ruskin's participation was a failure and he never completed the pillar left for him (to Bell Scott's delight).

A celebrated photograph of 1863 depicts Ruskin, Rossetti and Bell Scott together at Wallington. Such was his antipathy to Bell Scott, that Ruskin requested Lady Pauline to destroy the photograph, but she declined, and it now hangs in the ante-room to the Trevelyan bedroom.

Among Ruskin's voluminous works was the important *Time and Tide, by Weare and Tyne* (1867), twenty-five letters elucidating points in his utopian thinking. These letters were addressed to Thomas Dixon, the Sunderland working man who assisted Joseph Skipsey to recognition. The letters are gems of vigour, intelligence and force and are the best summary of Ruskin's social and economic ideas.

Ruskin, who used to visit Violet Hunt's parents at Crook Hall, thought the ensemble of river, cathedral and castle at Durham to be one of the seven wonders of the world.

Francis Scarfe (1911–1986)

Scarfe was born at 539 Stanhope Road, in South Shields, where he spent four years at the Royal Merchant Seaman's Orphanage, after his father was lost at sea in 1917. He recalled the military-type discipline (he was number 107), playing the bombardon (though unable to carry it to church), and exchanging notes through a wall with a girl he never met.

Scarfe attended the Boys High School in Shields, and subsequently Armstrong College Newcastle, Cambridge and the Sorbonne. By 1936 he was living in Paris, writing surrealist verse and attending meetings of the French Communist Party – both of which he abandoned in 1938. His published verse includes *Inscapes* (1940) and *Poems and Ballads* (1941) and also critical works like *Auden and After* (1942).

Following his war service he held academic posts in Glasgow, Paris and London, editing the Penguin *Baudelaire* in 1961. His poem 'Tyne Dock' recalls his 'shaggy mining town' with a sense of loss ('Tyne Dock Revisited' is unpublished), and 'In Memoriam' is a touching tribute to his mother:

> As you trailed through the Market together
> under the gas-jets, squeezing pennies
> to bid for bruised enormous oranges
>
> As guiding you into the future
> she told such marvels you forget about her
> whose hand held yours long after she was gone.

Sir Walter Scott (1771–1832)

In the summer of 1797, the young Walter Scott, his brother and a friend, made their headquarters in Gilsland, where the brothers became rivals for the attentions of Charlotte Mary Carpenter. After a whirlwind courtship, Scott proposed at the Popping Stone at Gilsland, and gave her purple pansies gathered on the Roman Wall. The marriage took place in Carlisle. The countryside here forms much of the background to Scott's novel *Guy Mannering*.

The future Laird of Abbotsford (formerly Clarty Hole) gained fame as a poet, particularly with *Marmion* (1808), before he began his career as a novelist. Flodden Field, near Ford Castle in Northumberland, where the Scots army was overthrown and King James IV killed in 1513, gave rise to verse on both sides of the border. Scott describes the scene in the sixth canto of *Marmion*. He gives credit to Robert Surtees, the celebrated Durham antiquary, for inspiring him to set about writing the epic at all. It includes an evocation of Northumberland:

> Then did the Alne attention claim,
> And Warkworth, proud of Percy's name;
> And next, they cross'd themselves, to hear
> The whitening breakers sound so near,
> Where, boiling through the rocks, they roar,
> On Dunstanborough's cavern'd shore;
> Thy tower, proud Bamborough, mark'd they there
> King Ida's castle, huge and square

The old ballad 'Durham Garland' provided the plot for Scott's novel *Guy Mannering* (1815) and in 'Harold the Dauntless', Scott addresses Durham Cathedral as 'Half Church of God, half castle 'gainst the Scot', which is inscribed on Prebends Bridge in Durham city. At the same time Scott expresses envy of Surtees' happier lot in living in such a place, rather than in Edinburgh.

Scott's first visit to Rokeby in June 1809 had him enthusing: 'The two most beautiful and rapid rivers of the north, Greta and Tees, join current in the demesne.' Mortham Tower and Eggleston Priory made a perfect romantic setting for a poem. Scott explored the villages of Teesdale – Winston, Scargill, Gainford and Brignall, and the moors beyond. Rokeby had been forfeited by its owners for supporting the king in the English Civil War and Scott's imagination kindled as he began another historical poem, *Rokeby*. By now, however, one may detect a certain over-casual facility in the verse.

On a second visit with his family to Rokeby three years later, Scott retired to a recess in the cliff face above the Greta and sat down to write at a rustic table with a reed surface. The scenes he described are still recognisable today. Scott had great difficulty in finishing the poem, but it was eventually published on New Year's Day 1813. It was, however, a failure, and ended Scott's career as poet. From then on, he devoted himself to the novel.

Scott visited Durham in 1827 to attend a banquet given by the Bishop in the castle hall for the Duke of Wellington. In the event, Scott too received a toast.

William Bell Scott (1811–1890)

Bell Scott, who resided at 14 St Thomas' Crescent in Newcastle, was the head of the Government Design School in the town from 1843–64. He was also involved in the Pre-Raphaelite movement and contributed to *The Germ*.

His work, particularly his celebrated *Iron and Coal*, can be seen in a famous set of murals celebrating North East history at Wallington Hall. In his *Autobiographical Notes*, Bell Scott tells us that he based this work on what he had witnessed in Stephenson's railway engine factory on Forth Street, behind Newcastle Central station: 'Entire wheels of welded iron were lifted out of the furnace red-hot and four giants, "strikers" as they were called, with mighty sledge hammers strode round them, striking in succession.' The inhabitants of Wallington Hall appear in the pictures, and the wielder of the hammer here is actually a portrait of Sir Charles Edward Trevelyan. Bell Scott himself appears helmeted in another picture, and Lady Pauline Trevelyan is among the women fleeing from the Danes. Scott also painted a set of panels at Wallington illustrating the famous ballad *Chevy Chase*.

It was at Wallington Hall in 1863 that Bell Scott was photographed with Rossetti and Ruskin, and where he first met Swinburne, who became a lifelong friend and frequent visitor to St Thomas' Crescent. Swinburne dedicated two poems to Scott.

Bell Scott's own poetry comprises odes, sonnets and mediaeval-style ballads. He is well represented in the *Oxford Book of Victorian Verse*.

Anya Seton (1904–1990)

Anya Seton was the daughter of Ernest Thompson Seton. A well-known historical novelist living in America, she produced best-sellers in *Dragonwyck* (1941), which was made into a film starring Gene Tierney and Vincent Price, and *Foxfire* (1950), filmed with Jane Russell and Jeff Chandler.

Her novel *Devil Water* (1962) concerns James, the luckless Earl of Derwentwater of Dilston Hall, near Hexham and his involvement with the Jacobite rising of 1715. She also narrates the story of his brother Charles, beheaded after the 1745 rebellion (the last man to die for the cause). The action of the novel moves back and forth between Northumberland, Tyneside, London and America. General Tom Forster and his sister Dorothy, who assisted him to escape from his London jail, both make an appearance, along with members of well-known border families like the Widdringtons and Collingwoods.

Anya Seton states that the book developed out of her love for Northumberland – from Tyneside, where her father was born in South Shields, to the Scottish Border where many of her ancestors came from (there is a story that she was descended from George Seton, the last Earl of Winton). Her grandmother was a Snowdon, and Anya certainly visited her Snowdon cousins at Felton. Billy Pigg, the celebrated Northumbrian piper played 'Derwentwater's Farewell' specially for her. The novel shows thorough research of events and places, though the accents are perhaps a little wayward!

Anya Seton said that her greatest debt of all was to Miss Amy Flagg of Westoe Village in South Shields, who provided her with much documentation and information.

Ernest Thompson Seton (1860–1946)

He was born Ernest Evan Seton Thompson at 43, Beach Road, South Shields, where there is a plaque on a tree in the garden outside. The family, which included twelve sons, emigrated to Canada in 1866.

Seton gained experience as a naturalist by trailing and hunting in the prairie country of Manitoba in the last years of the nineteenth century. He used this knowledge as the basis for his animal stories, and his artistic training enabled him to illustrate his own books. His most popular work was *Wild Animals I Have Known* (1898) but he wrote on until the 1940s.

Seton fought for the establishment of reservations for the Indians, and parks for threatened animal species. He later became chairman of the committee which established the Boy Scouts of America. As well as further books on scouting and woodcraft, he wrote an autobiography, *The Trail of an Artist-Naturalist*, published in 1940.

Seton's writings on woodcraft greatly influenced Lord Baden-Powell in setting up the Boy Scout movement, and later admirers have included Gavin Maxwell and Richard Adams, who acknowledges the influence of his books on *Watership Down*, the best-selling rabbit saga of recent years.

William Shakespeare (1564–1616)

The Percy family reigned in Northumbeland as virtual kings after 1309, and conducted hostilities along the frontier with Scotland at times almost as a family affair. Alnwick Castle, which became their fortress, is the largest inhabited castle in the country, after Windsor Castle. Alnwick saw the death of the Scottish king, Malcolm III, in 1093 during his fifth invasion of England. This is Shakespeare's Malcolm, who appears in *Macbeth*.

In *Richard II*, one of Shakespeare's finest works, Henry Percy, 1st Earl of Northumberland, has a significant role in placing the usurper Bolingbroke on the throne of England as Henry IV. Percy's son, Harry, known as Hotspur for his reckless courage, also makes a brief appearance.

The next play in Shakespeare's great historical sequence is *Henry IV (Part One)*. By now, Henry Percy had come to feel ill-rewarded for his service against the Scots on the northern border and for his help in making Henry IV king. Besides this, the Percys distrusted the king's reliance on the hated Neville family. Meanwhile, Harry Hotspur had distinguished himself in battle against the French and the Scots, and it is he who plays a major role in Shakespeare's drama.

Several characters contrast Hotspur favourably with the king's son, Prince Hal, the future Henry V. Shakespeare in fact altered Hotspur's real age to make him as young as Prince Hal. The latter wastes his time in pranks among the low-born, while the spirited Hotspur extravagantly declares:

> By heaven, methinks it were an easy leap
> To pluck bright honour from the pale-fac'd moon.

Hal envies him his valour, but intends, by killing him, to make his own reputation. Shakespeare indicates that the chivalrous Hotspur is not calculating enough to be a king, while Hal alienates our sympathy by being just that. Certainly the future hero of Agincourt never enjoys the charming domestic scenes that Shakespeare gives Hotspur and his wife Kate at Warkworth castle.

After Hotspur's death on 21 July 1403, at a place north of Shrewsbury, still called Battlefield, the play ends. *Henry IV (Part Two)* opens at Warkworth Castle, where Hotspur's widow and parents discuss plans and the Earl of Northumberland leaves for Scotland. Historically, Henry IV's forces reduced the great Northumberland fortresses without trouble, Warkworth becoming the first English castle to fall to artillery. There is nothing of this in the play, however, which is elegiac in mood and looks backward a good deal: Richard II, and Hotspur himself are both recalled.

The gallant Hotspur is commemorated in the gate that bears his name at Alnwick, while the stiff-tailed Percy lion can be seen on Warkworth Castle and on the bridge at Alnwick Castle. It also stands (in lead) on top of Syon House at the Northumberland seat on the Thames in outer London. A façade in Northumberland Street in Newcastle bears the effigies of four men eminent in the region's history. One of them is Harry Hotspur.

Later Earls of Northumberland had a chequered history. The second and third were killed during the Wars of the Roses, and the fourth was murdered. The seventh was beheaded in 1572 and the eighth found shot in the Tower in 1585, where the ninth Earl spent fifteen years as a prisoner. The tenth Earl fought against Charles I in the Civil War and then helped in the Restoration of the monarchy.

But from the times of Hotspur and his successors in the Earldom –
'The Magnificent'; 'The Unthrifty'; 'The Wizard' – whether uphold-
ing the crown or opposing it, the name of Percy was always one to
reckon with.

The Wars of the Roses may be said to have started with a skirmish
between the Percys and the Nevilles at Stamford Bridge in Yorkshire
in 1453, and Shakespeare devotes no fewer than three plays to the
troubled reign of Henry VI. However, though the sweet-natured king
ruled England in name from Bamburgh Castle in 1464, and his
indomitable wife Margaret, 'the she-wolf of France', lived on a
herring a day after the disaster at Hexham in that year, the playwright's attentions lie elsewhere. The sardonic figure of the Duke of
York's son Richard, grows ever more formidable, until he dominates
his own play, *Richard III*.

Richard, like his brother Edward IV, was a son of Cicely Neville,
'the Rose of Raby', and Richard Plantagenet, Duke of York. The fine
alabaster tomb of Richard's maternal grandparents is in the church
at Staindrop, near the magnificent Neville seat at Raby Castle.
According to the *Shell Guide to Durham*, Wordsworth wrote:

> Seven hundred knights, retainers all
> Of Neville at their master's call
> Had sate together in Raby's Hall

By the time of the Wars of the Roses, the Nevilles had become the
greatest family in the realm. The Earl of Warwick ('the kingmaker')
was a nephew of Cicely Neville, and has an important role in
Shakespeare's Plantagenet plays.

Richard usually resided at Middleham Castle in North Yorkshire,
where he had spent most of his childhood, and where annual celebrations in his honour are held. He was generally popular in the north,
which he ruled for his royal brother and, though tough and
unscrupulous enough, was not the monster described by
Shakespeare; nor was he noticeably deformed. During his brother's
reign, Richard was often in Newcastle, as he had a grant of the castle
there. He successfully invaded Scotland in 1482 and was responsible
for the final capture of Berwick upon Tweed, after the town had
changed hands, or been sacked, some fourteen times over the previous three centuries.

Granville Sharp (1735–1813)

Sharp was the ninth son of the rector of Rothbury and archdeacon
of Northumberland, Thomas Sharp, himself a prolific writer of theological works. Born in Durham and educated at the grammar school
there, Granville Sharp acquired scholarly tastes and taught himself
Greek and Hebrew; by 1770, he had published a number of works of
biblical criticism.

He eventually became active in the anti-slavery movement and
defended a black immigrant, James Somerset. It was entirely owing
to Sharp's efforts that the famous legal decision of 1772 was
obtained, that as soon as any slave sets foot in England, he or she
becomes free.

Sharp joined the crusade against the press-gangs as well as working
with Thomas Clarkson for the abolition of slavery; his suggestion for

a home for freed slaves in Sierra Leone was adopted. He was a founder of the British and Foreign Bible Society and also wrote many legal, political and theological pamphlets, as well as historical treatises. He was active in the study of language too, and one of his tracts, *Remarks on the Use of the Definitive article in the Greek text of the New Testament* published in 1798, proposed the rule known as 'Granville Sharp's canon'. Because of its important bearing on Unitarian doctrine, this gave rise to a celebrated controversy in which many leading churchmen took part, including Christopher Wordsworth.

Sharp became the father-figure of the celebrated Clapham sect of philanthropists and evangelicals, who included William Wilberforce, Henry Thornton and Zachary Macaulay, the father of Lord Macaulay. Sharp is commemorated in Westminster Abbey.

George Bernard Shaw (1856–1950)

In the first issue of *The Savoy* in January 1896, Bernard Shaw (as he always preferred to be called), describes a visit to St George's, Jesmond in the early 1890s, while out walking in what he calls 'a polite suburb of Newcastle'. He was much impressed, but got little change out of the Geordie verger, who responded to every question put to him by this probing Irishman with the information that Mr Spence (the architect) was responsible. Shaw felt that the church decoration was so beautiful there ought to have been more of it.

Shaw also had theatrical links with Newcastle. His *Caesar and Cleopatra*, for example, was given its copyright performance on 15 March 1899 at the Theatre Royal by Mrs Patrick Campbell's company.

Early in 1921, Shaw was invited to visit the People's Theatre, of which he was a supporter, in its new premises in the Royal Arcade in Pilgrim Street. The dramatist, however, said he would not travel to Newcastle in February to see the Day of Judgment, let alone *Man and Superman*, affecting to take the invitation as an indirect attempt on his life. He did arrive in April, however, and when the audience called for him to speak after the play, he stood up and said that they had been listening to Shaw for three hours and if that wasn't enough, he couldn't hope to satisfy them – and sat down again. Asked his opinion of the performance, the sage simply remarked: 'Infamous' – though if that was really true, the difficulties he had himself placed in the way of the production were largely responsible.

The grassy mound where Rye Hill ends marks the site where, in 1936, at the age of 80, Shaw made his final appearance on any stage at the end of the People's Theatre performance of his play *Candida*. Shaw spoke for about fifteen minutes and declared that for his last performance there was no theatre he would rather be in.

Percy Bysshe Shelley (1792–1822)

Just as John Lilburne was the best loved man in England in his day, so Lord Eldon (born in Love Lane, Newcastle) became the most hated man in his. During the wars with revolutionary France, William Pitt and Eldon, his Chancellor, were concerned to stamp out any sign of what they regarded as sedition. Eldon was prime minister in all but name for long periods, and change of any kind became anathema to him. Shelley wrote scathing verses against him in 1817, beginning:

Thy country's curse is on thee, darkest crest
Of that foul, knotted, many-headed worm
Which rends our mother's bosom . . .

Shelley, incidentally, travelled through the North East via Newcastle in 1811 on the way to marry Harriet Westbrook in Edinburgh.

Eldon, for his part, was not widely read. Given a copy of Milton's *Paradise Lost*, he was asked later what he thought of the character of Satan. Eldon replied: 'Damn fine fellow, I hope he wins!'

Matthew Phipps Shiel (1865–1947)

A fantasy writer of considerable stylistic interest, Shiel produced his masterpiece *The Purple Cloud* in 1901. In it, the explorer Adam Jeffson returns from the North Pole to find mammalian life has been exterminated by a volcanic gas. Jeffson's home is said to be near Rokeby, and the surrounding district is described in some topographical detail. Jeffson indeed spends three hours brooding at the top of the fortress in Barnard Castle.

The narrative goes on to describe, in brilliantly vivid prose, Jeffson's frantic search for survivors down mines all over the country, including the Yorkshire Dales, Alston Moor and Allendale. The mine descriptions and the obsessive tone of the writing in this section of the novel are oddly reminiscent of Auden's fascination with lead mining in the same area some 20 years later.

Simeon of Durham (fl 1096–1129)

Simeon was a precentor of the monastery of Durham and his work is a principal source of Anglo-Norman history. Bede supplied the first part of Simeon's history: from the end of Bede's *Historia*, Simeon relied on a Northumbrian chronicle, now lost, and the work of Florence of Worcester. Simeon's work, whether as writer or editor, is of great value.

After the Norman conquest, rebellion had to be suppressed in the North. 'The Harrying of the North' is described by Simeon of Durham as follows:

In consequence of the Normans having plundered . . . principally Northumbria and the adjacent provinces, so great a famine prevailed that men, compelled by hunger, devoured human flesh, that of horses, dogs and cats, and whatever custom abhors . . . Meanwhile, the land being thus deprived of anyone to cultivate it for nine years, an extensive solitude prevailed all round. There was no village inhabited between York and Durham; they became lurking places for wild beast and robbers, and were a great dread to travellers.

Joseph Skipsey (1832–1903)

The collier poet was born in the Percy parish of Tynemouth, where his father was shot dead in a clash between pitmen and special constables. Skipsey himself worked in the pits from the age of seven; he had no schooling, but taught himself to read and write. In 1852, he walked most of the way to London, found work on the railways, married his landlady and returned north to work in Scotland, and later at Choppington and the Pembroke collieries near Sunderland.

In 1859 he published a volume of *Poems* in Morpeth, though this seems not to be extant. It attracted the attention of the editor of the *Gateshead Observer*, James Clephan, who obtained a job for him as under store-keeper at Hawks, Crawshay and Son in Gateshead. In 1863, after a fatal accident to one of his children in the works, he moved to Newcastle where Robert Spence Watson had secured him a position as asssistant librarian to the Literary and Philosophical Society. The work did not suit him, however, and the pay was none too good. He returned to the mines the following year to work for various companies till 1882. Skipsey became part of Robert Spence Watson's wide circle of acquaintance; his table talk is said to have been trenchant and to the point.

In 1883 he delivered his lecture, 'The Poet as Seer and Singer' to the Literary and Philosophical Society in Newcastle and subsequently published a number of books, including *Carols from the Coalfields* (1886), drawing praise from Rossetti and Oscar Wilde, who likened the poems to those of William Blake.

From September 1888 to June 1889, Skipsey was a caretaker at Durham College of Physical Science, Newcastle, a position arranged by Spence Watson, and was then appointed custodian of Shakespeare's birthplace at Stratford-on-Avon on the recommendation of Burne-Jones, Tennyson, Rossetti, Bram Stoker and other eminent men. He resigned two years later, and the episode gave rise to Henry James' story 'The Birthplace'. Skipsey returned north and died at Harraton in 1903.

Basil Bunting contributes an interesting preface to the Ceolfrith Press edition of Skipsey's selected poems (Sunderland, 1976). In comparing Skipsey to Burns, he makes the telling point that the Scot saw Ayr and Dumfries vividly, but from outside. Skipsey was so much inside the pit village, he hardly notices Cowpen or Percy Main at all.

Dignified and austere as a man, Skipsey could be windy and rhetorical as a writer. He is at his best when describing his own experience as a pitman. Rossetti called him: 'Joseph Skipsey, the Northern Collier Poet, a man of real genius.' This poem Rossetti considered to equal to anything in the language for quietly direct pathos:

'*Get Up!*'

'Get up!' the caller calls, 'Get up!'
And in the dead of night,
To win the bairns their bite and sup,
I rise a weary wight.

My flannel duddon donn'd, thrice o'er
My birds are kiss'd, and then
I with a whistle shut the door,
I may not ope again.

Christopher Smart (1722–1771)

Smart attended Durham School in the 1730s, and came to the notice of Henrietta, Duchess of Cleveland, of Raby Castle. She invited him to the castle, secured his entry to Cambridge in 1739 and gave him a pension.

Robert Browning in his *Parleyings with Certain People Important in their Day* (1887) includes Charles Avison, the celebrated Newcastle composer and organist, and Christopher Smart among the pegs he hangs his own reflections on (the conversations are entirely one-sided). Browning was one of Smart's few nineteenth century admirers – in fact, he seems to regard Smart's as the greatest achievement between Milton and Keats:

> Smart, solely of such songmen, pierced the screen
> Twixt thing and word, lit language straight from soul, –
> Left no fine film-flake on the naked coal

and states later that Smart, at least on one occasion:

> Had reached the zenith from his madhouse cell.

Smart suffered from insanity after 1756, though Doctor Johnson for one did not think he ought to be confined. 'His infirmities were not noxious to society. He insisted on people praying with him and I'd as lief pray with Kit Smart as anyone else. Another charge laid was that he did not love clean linen; and I have no passion for it.' In his crusty old age, however, the Doctor compared a choice between Derrick and Smart as one between a louse and a flea!

Smart was confined intermittently to an asylum in London between 1756 and 1763, during which time he produced his astonishing *Jubilate Agno*. Among much else that is rich and strange, including the endearing description of his cat Jeoffrey, there is a reference to Staindrop Moor:

> For I bless God the Postmaster General and all conveyancers
> of letters under his care especially Allen and Shelvock.
> For my grounds in New Canaan shall infinitely compensate
> for the flats and maynes of Staindrop Moor.

Tobias Smollett (1721–1771)

Smollett, the prejudiced and irascible Scottish novelist, was satirised by Laurence Sterne as 'the learned Smelfungus', after the publication of his scathing travel book on France and Italy. David Hume, who knew him better, considered him to be a cocoanut, rough only on the outside.

In his best novel, *The Expedition of Humphry Clinker*, Smollet has his characters travel north to Scotland, as he himself did in the 1760s, via Durham and Newcastle. Smollett was a hard man to impress:

> The city of Durham appears like a confused heap of stones and brick, accumulated so as to cover a mountain, round which a river winds its brawling course. The streets are generally narrow, dark and unpleasant, and many of them almost impassable in consequence of their declivity. The cathedral is a huge gloomy pile . . .

Newcastle comes off even worse. Smollett had been here in May 1766, when Wesley was preaching; in the novel, Tabitha Bramble attends a Wesley meeting. The book also tells of how some wag in Newcastle terrified the servants by saying that there was nothing to eat in Scotland except oat-meal and sheep's heads! Smollett clearly knew his way round town: in his novel *Roderick Random*, the hero is recognised by his old school-friend Strap, who is working for the proprietor in a barber's shop in Pilgrim Street.

Of Northumberland, Smollett remarks, not without a tinge of patriotic glee, that the English side of the Tweed is less prosperous than the Scottish, testifying to the formidable presence of the Scots in days gone by.

Thomas Spence (1750–1814)

The diminutive Spence, who taught elementary English in the Broad Chare, was born on the Newcastle Quayside on 21 June 1750. An acquaintance of Bewick, he probably had some contact with Marat during the latter's visit to Newcastle in 1775, at the short-lived Philosophical Society in Westgate Street, where Spence put forward his scheme for the public ownership of land. This caused his ejection from the society, whose members disapproved of its 'levelling' tendencies. Spence was also concerned to support the rights of mothers and children – as well as promoting a phonetic alphabet, in which several of his works were published. This scheme is expounded in his *Grand Repository of the English Language*. His pamphlet, *The Meridian Sun of Liberty* was hawked around Newcastle and appeared in London in 1793.

Spence had travelled to London in 1792, where he opened a book stall. With the French Revolution in full swing across the Channel, William Pitt and his Lord Chancellor, Eldon, were concerned to stamp out any sign of what was seen as sedition. The days when Eldon had eloped with Bessie Surtees through a first-floor window in Sandhill were long gone and Spence was arrested for selling copies of Tom Paine's *Rights of Man*. Acquitted, he went on with his perilous trade in handbills and a magazine called *Pig's Meat* (1793–96), a reference to Edmund Burke's disparaging remark about the swinish multitude. He was imprisoned three times before 1795, arrested in 1798, and in jail again in 1801, but the small Spencean society, reorganised as the Society of Spencean Philanthropists, continued to be a centre for agitation until and beyond Spence's death on 8 September 1814. They were finally suppressed in 1820. Harriet Martineau gives some account of their activities in her *England During the Thirty Years Peace*.

Spence's thought influenced Robert Owen, and later socialists through him. His basic political plan, developed in a series of pamphlets from 1783 onwards, is set out in his *Constitution of Spensonia, A Country in Fairyland, situated between Utopia and Oceana, brought from thence by Captain Swallow*, which came out in three editions in 1803. The epilogue ends endearingly:

> For who can tell but the Millennium
> May take its rise from my poor Cranium? . . .

Christina Stead (1902–1983)

Christina Stead, the 'dark star' of Australian literature, set her only English novel, *Cotters' England* (1966) partly in Gateshead (called Bridgehead). Her reputation has risen greatly in recent years and most of her works have been published by Virago Press.

She was in Newcastle in the summer of 1949, accompanied by her friend Anne Dooley (nee Kelly), a Geordie girl, who was the model for Nellie Cotter, the extraordinary heroine of the book. Anne was no doubt responsible for Stead's reasonable attempt at conveying the local accent.

The novelist's plan was to visit the towns around Newcastle as well, but though many of these are mentioned by name in the book – as are the High Level Bridge (admiringly) and even Two Ball Lonnen in Newcastle – there is no attempt to convey the historical, cultural, industrial or even political background of the region; this is somewhat surprising in one as politically committed as Stead. At all events, one gets none of the strong sense of place which distinguishes Tyneside, nor the warmth and humour of the Geordies; her view of the region is grim and downbeat. The summer of 1949 was hot, but the weather in Bridgehead is a raw February, with plenty of soot and drizzle to match Stead's vision of her characters (the revealing American title of the book is *Dark Places of the Heart*).

It appears that the house she stayed in was a tedious walk up the hill from Gateshead station: the Kelly family with the right names lived at 37, South Street (now demolished) opposite the school.

William Thomas Stead (1849–1912)

Stead, one of the most outstanding and influential of late Victorian figures, was born in the manse at Embleton in Northumberland. He then lived from 1849 to 1861 in the end house in Church Street, Howdon. The house has been demolished to make way for the Howdon tunnel. Stead was apprenticed in 1863 and spent some seven years in the counting-house of a wine and spirit merchant at 27 Broad Chare, Newcastle. In the early 1870s he began writing articles for the newly-founded *Northern Echo* in Darlington, which were of such quality that he was made editor in April 1871 – without any previous journalistic experience. The stone where Stead used to tether his horse can be seen in Crown Street, Darlington.

In 1873 he married Lucy Wilson of Howdon and in 1880 began his celebrated association with the *Pall Mall Gazette* in London. As its dynamic editor in 1883, he became a fearless and influential supporter of causes, as he pioneered what Matthew Arnold called 'the new journalism'. He gained great notoriety in July 1885, when he purchased a child prostitute in order to expose a vile trade in a series of articles entitled 'The Maiden Tribute of Modern Babylon'. This led indirectly to prison for Stead (and the raising of the age of consent from 12 to 16). He was a vigorous campaigner for international peace and was nominated for the Nobel Peace Prize in 1901.

Stead was greatly interested in psychical research and, it seems, had been told he would never die by water. Ironically, he perished in the *Titanic* disaster of 1912. Courageous and unselfish to the end, he was last seen helping women and children to escape. There are no fewer than four plaques to Stead in England, including those at Embleton and Darlington (but none on Tyneside).

Percival Stockdale (1736–1811)

Born in Branxton, Northumberland, Stockdale spent six years at Alnwick Grammar School, then moved on to school in Berwick.

Stockdale never doubted that he had poetic genius, but this view was not shared by the public.

Stockdale served in Admiral Byng's expedition to Minorca in 1756. On his way back to his mother at Berwick, he stayed in Durham and was there persuaded to enter the church. He was ordained in 1759. Working in London, Stockdale mixed with the literary figures of the day, including Doctor Johnson and Garrick. Boswell remarks that Johnson, after one of his pamphlets had been coldly received, 'was soothed in the highest strain of panegyrick, in a poem called "The Remonstrance" by the Rev. Mr Stockdale, to whom he was, upon many occasions, a kind protector.'

Stockdale eventually received the living of Lesbury and Longhoughton in Northumberland in 1783. There he published a five-act tragedy *Ximenes* (1788), and much varied material, including *Thirteen Sermons to Seamen; Poetical Thoughts and Views on the Banks of the Wear*; an amusing correspondence with the Bishop of Durham, Shute Barrington; and a remonstrance against the cruel sport of bull-baiting. Stockdale's *Poems* were published in 1808 and his interesting *Memoirs* in 1809. In the latter, he was still expressing his yearnings for literary immortality. He died at Lesbury on 4 September 1811.

Marie Stopes (1870–1958)

Best known for her work in the field of birth control, Dr Stopes wrote a good deal in various genres and produced 70 works, including plays, fairy tales and novels. In July 1914, after her disastrous first marriage, she set out to live in a tent on the Northumberland coast near Longhoughton, in order to rest, write poetry and sort out her life. This was at the invitation of Lord Grey of Howick, the nephew of Sir Edward Grey the then Foreign Secretary. It may be that she knew the area from her youth in Edinburgh.

At all events, she had rather a hard time roughing it, despite letters (and apples) from Aylmer Maude, the great Russian translator. She was grateful for dinner at Howick on one occasion. Unlike the Webbs, she appears not to have had the best of weather, and the outbreak of war brought intrusive soldiery. At all events, she was back in London in September.

It is curious to think that some 30 miles away at this time, E. M. Forster was visiting the Turners, near Duns, in Berwickshire. The house guests, including Ford Madox Ford and Violet Hunt, were awaiting the arrival of Wyndham Lewis. On his rail journeys, Lewis must have passed within two miles of Dr Stopes' tent.

In 1952, she befriended Avro Manhattan, the handsome poet and artist. Though at 39 he was far younger than her, he was no doubt flattered, and they saw a good deal of one another. The friendship did not last, however, and she made him no bequest in her will.

Robert Surtees (1779–1834)

The celebrated antiquary was born in South Bailey, in Durham city and lived at Mainsforth Hall, just off the road from Bishop Middleham to Ferryhill. As an undergraduate at Oxford, Surtees dreamed of writing a history of Durham and it was to this that he devoted his life. He used to drive around the country with a groom in attendance, examining all remains of antiquity, noting inscriptions and other documents. According to his friend, John Raine, his groom would complain that it was 'weary work' for 'we could never get past an auld beelding.'

Surtees suffered almost continual ill-health which meant that the great work was written paragraph by laborious paragraph. The *History of Durham* contains an enormous amount of genealogical information, no doubt because his position enabled Surtees to see many family deeds and documents. There is humour too, unexpected in such a work, and fragments of his own poetry.

Surtees was a friend of Sir Walter Scott (who visited Mainsforth in April 1809) and passed off a ballad of his own on the great man as genuine. This was 'The Death of Featherstonehaugh' which described the feud between the Featherstones and the Ridleys. It even found a place in the *Minstrelsy of the Scottish Border* with notes by both Scott and Surtees! Surtees always kept quiet about this for fear of hurting Scott. He also wrote the words of 'Derwentwater's Farewell', a favourite with players of the Northumbrian small pipes. The sad story of the young earl's fatal involvement with the Jacobite rebellion begins:

> Farewell to pleasant Dilston Hall
> My father's ancient seat,

and ends:

> Oh! Carry me to Northumberland,
> In my father's grave to lie.

Surtees lived as much as possible in the quiet seclusion of Mainsforth Hall, where he kept an open house for people who shared his interests. He died on 15 February 1834 (Southey was present at the funeral) and his memorial is in Bishop Middleham church. The Surtees Society was founded in 1834 to carry on his work.

Overcome, as Henry Thorold puts it in the *Shell Guide*, by proximity to Ferryhill and coal, Mainsforth Hall was demolished in 1962. Only the gate piers survive.

Robert Smith Surtees (1803–1864)

Robert Surtees attended school in Ovingham and Durham before being articled in 1822 to Robert Purvis, a solicitor in Market Street, Newcastle. At that time Market Street was next to the old Theatre Royal, now submerged by Grey Street.

He left for London in 'the genial spring of 1825' by the old Highflyer coach at eight in the morning from Newcastle, having risen at Hamsterley Hall between five and six. Surtees had intended to practise law in the capital but had trouble making his way in his profession and began contributing to the *Sporting Magazine*. He launched out on his own with the *New Sporting Magazine* in 1831, contributing the comic papers which appeared as *Jorrocks' Jaunts and Jollities* in 1838.

Jorrocks, the sporting cockney grocer with his vulgarity and good-natured artfulness was a great success with the public and Surtees produced more Jorrocks novels in the same vein, notably *Handley Cross* (which gives its name to a bridge at Hamsterley) and *Hillingdon Hall*, where the description of the house is very reminiscent of

Hamsterley. Another hero, Mr Soapey Sponge, appears in *Mr Sponge's Sporting Tour*, possibly Surtees' best work. All Surtees' novels were composed at Hamsterley Hall, where he wrote standing up at a desk, like Victor Hugo.

In 1835, Surtees abandoned his legal practice and, after he inherited Hamsterley Hall in 1838, devoted himself to hunting and shooting, meanwhile writing anonymously for his own pleasure. He was a major in the Durham militia and became High Sheriff of Durham in 1856. He died in Brighton in 1864 and was buried in Ebchester church.

Though Surtees did not set his novels in any readily identifiable locality, he uses North East place-names like Sheepwash, Howell (How) Burn and Winford Rig. His memorable Geordie, James Pigg, in *Handley Cross*, bespeaks a knowledge of North East speech and manners which will raise a smile:

> 'Vere d'ye come from?'
>
> 'Cannynewcassel,' replied Pigg. 'Ar's a native of Paradise aside Cannynewcassel – ye'll ken Cannynewcassel, nae doubt,' observed he, running the words together . . . 'Ye see, John Pigg willed away arl wore brass to the Formory, ye see and left me wi' fairly nout. Gin ye gan to the Newcastle Formory, ye'll see arle aboot it, in great goud letters, clagged against the walls.'

As a creator of comical personalities, Surtees is still very readable today. Thackeray envied his power of characterisation, while William Morris considered him 'a master of life' and ranked him with Dickens. The novels are engaging and vigorous, and abound in sharp social observation, with a keener eye than Dickens for the natural world. Perhaps Surtees most resembles the Dickens of *Pickwick Papers* which, we recall, was originally intended as mere supporting matter for a series of sporting illustrations to rival Jorrocks.

Algernon Swinburne (1837–1909)

Swinburne, though born in London, was early removed from it and disliked it throughout his life. The son of an admiral, he was brought up in the Isle of Wight, but spent a good deal of the year at Capheaton Hall. He considered Northumberland to be his native county, 'the crowning county of England – yes, the best!' There he stayed with his grandfather, Sir John Swinburne (1762–1860), who survived trepanning after a shooting accident to live to be nearly 100. Sir John had a famous library and was President of the Literary and Philosophical Society in Newcastle until 1837. Swinburne used to ride his pony over to Cambo, where the perpetual curate, John Wilkinson, prepared him somewhat desultorily for entry to Eton. 'He was too clever and would never study,' complained the curate.

Despite Swinburne's later fame as a poet, it is in his novel *Lesbia Brandon* that we find the spell of the north at its strongest. The splendid landscape and seascape – what Swinburne called 'the joyful and fateful beauty of the seas off Bamborough' – are certainly Northumbrian, and Herbert's exhilarating contact with the sea mirrors that pain which for Swinburne was notoriously inseparable from pleasure. Swinburne's abiding love for the region (his favourite word for the north is 'bright') is memorably reflected in poems like the intensely patriotic 'Northumberland', as well as 'Grace Darling', 'The Tyneside Widow', 'Winter in Northumberland' and 'A Jacobite's Exile', with its haunting evocation of the Till, the Wansbeck and the Tyne. William Bell Scott's striking portrait of Swinburne, painted against the background of the Northumberland coast, hangs in Balliol College at Oxford. The drawings for this were made during a trip the pair made to Grace Darling's Longstones lighthouse on the Farne Islands in 1859.

In the years 1857–60, Swinburne became one of Lady Pauline Trevelyan's intellectual circle at Wallington Hall, which he recalls in a poem of 1882 to William Bell Scott as 'that bright household in our joyous north'. Indeed, the dominant old lady character in his novel *Love's Cross-Currents* is said to be based on Lady Pauline. Ernest Radworth is believed to be her husband, Sir Walter Trevelyan. Somewhat eccentric, Sir Walter once found a Balzac novel that Swinburne had left on the drawing-room table, and threw it on the fire in disgust. Swinburne was outraged and walked out of the house.

When his father was displeased at his failing to take a degree at Oxford, Swinburne withdrew again northwards to Capheaton. After his grandfather's death in 1860, he stayed with the Bell Scotts at 14, St Thomas Crescent in Newcastle, lying before the fire, surrounded by books resembling a ruined fortress. Scott recalls holding Swinburne's head while a Newcastle dentist removed a 'mighty grinder' bit by bit, noting that the poet was almost indifferent to the pain.

In December 1862, close on Christmas, Swinburne arrived in St Thomas' Crescent, hot-foot from Wallington and proceeded to accompany Bell Scott and his guests on a trip from Newcastle to Tynemouth. Scott writes that as they walked by the sea, the poet declaimed the 'Hymn to Proserpine' and 'Laus Veneris' in his strange intonation while the waves were 'running the whole length of the long level sands towards Cullercoats and sounding like far-off acclamations'.

In London, Rossetti was delighted with his 'little Northumbrian friend'. Swinburne was indeed small, though no weakling, and his red head was disproportionately large, making him something of an odd figure. His behaviour was certainly disconcerting; at 30, he knelt down to read a poem to Mazzini. Rossetti, dismayed that Swinburne was hiring flagellants to beat him, paid an actress £10 to bring him back to the sexual straight and narrow: the effort was a failure and she returned the money. Swinburne was not above writing about such things, however, his fantasy *La Soeur de la Reine* imagines what few others would – Wordsworth seducing Queen Victoria.

Swinburne is out of fashion nowadays. T. S. Eliot's attack on his romantic vagueness was too devastating for most, while others are still disturbed by hymns to flagellation and necrophilia. Swinburne's first poems had suggested that nothing might be beyond him, but despite the occasional intoxicating brilliance of his technique, he never grew out of his romantic youth. It is poignant all the same to think of the former devotee of liberty, the lover of sea and moorland, wrecked by his excesses and kept under (strictly sober) supervision by his friend Watts-Dunton at 'The Pines' in Putney for the last 30 years of his life.

Cecil Philip Taylor (1929–1981)

Cecil Taylor was born in Glasgow and came to Newcastle, the city where his mother had grown up, in 1955 as a travelling salesman. He married a Glaswegian girl in 1956 and lived in Newcastle at 30 Lindale Road, Fenham, for many years.

His first play was *Aa Went to Blaydon Races* (1962) while *Peter Pan Man* transfers the famous play to an Elswick estate in Newcastle's west end. The Live Theatre in Newcastle premiered his *Bandits* (1977), which was also performed by the Royal Shakespeare Company. *Operation Elvis* was televised by the BBC. His most successful work was probably *Good* (1981) in which a liberal German professor's moral cowardice leads to his involvement with the Nazi war machine and Auschwitz.

The Tyne Tees production of *And a Nightingale Sang*, a bitter-sweet comedy set on wartime Tyneside, won a Prix Europa in 1990. Taylor's drama has also featured as a central theme of the Edinburgh Festival: several plays have recently been published by Methuen under the title *North*.

Cecil Taylor was the founding spirit of the Northern Playwrights' Society (which still flourishes) and several of his plays for Live Theatre have been brought out by the North East publisher, Iron Press.

Taylor lived in various parts of Northumberland with his second wife, eventually settling in Longhorsley, near Morpeth. His untimely death, apparently from bronchial pneumonia, has been attributed to his habit of writing in his garden shed.

Sir Henry Taylor (1800–1886)

Taylor was born in Bishop Middleham, the son of a gentleman farmer, and spent his youth in Witton-le-Wear with his stepmother at Witton Hall (now Witton Tower) in the High Street. His father George was a friend of Wordsworth and the poet visited him at Witton in July 1938. Mrs Taylor was a cousin of Miss Fenwick, who was travelling with Wordsworth, and it was through his stepmother that Henry became acquainted with Wordsworth and Southey.

In Witton, Henry wrote 'The Cave of Ceada' which was accepted for the *Quarterly Review*. Another poem, 'The Lynnburn' is about the river which runs through the village. He became editor of the *London Magazine* in 1823, and from 1824 to 1872 he worked in the Colonial Office as an administrator. Taylor wrote a number of plays, including *Isaac Comnenus* (1827) and *Philip van Artevelde* (1834), and in 1845 there followed a book of lyrical poems. His essay *The Statesman* (1836) caused some controversy, being a satirical view of how the civil service really works. He published his *Autobiography* in 1885, which contains pleasant portraits of Wordsworth, Southey, Tennyson and Scott among others.

John Taylor (?1578–1653)

'The Water-Poet' arrived in Newcastle on 1 October 1618 in the course of his *Penniless Pilgrimage* – a round trip to Scotland from

London, without spending a penny on food or lodging. Taylor was a wag, who once set out on a short-lived trip in a boat made of brown paper, and using stock-fish on canes as oars. His works too, often have freakish titles like *A Very Merry Wherry Ferry Voyage*. The verse is usually little more than doggerel, but amusing enough.

Sir Henry Widdrington, a fellow old soldier met him in Newcastle and gave him a horse out of gratitude for Taylor's saving him from starvation in the Azores. Taylor also says he was welcomed at Master Nicholas Tempest's house. This was no doubt Stella Hall. It was a rambling Elizabethan building in Taylor's time, later converted into an eighteenth century house by James Paine. The house was demolished in 1955; only the fine octagonal gazebo remains standing roofless on Summerhouse Hill.

Tom Taylor (1817–1880)

Taylor, by turns dramatist, editor and critic, was born the son of a brewer in Bishopwearmouth (Sunderland). His father's business was in Horn's Lane, off High Street East and the family lived in High Street West, just south of the Wearmouth Bridge.

Taylor became Professor of English at London University, 1845–47 and later editor of *Punch* from 1874 until his death in 1880. He wrote some 80 plays in his lifetime as well as much journalism. Between 1853 and 1870, he was house dramatist at the Olympic, and later the Haymarket theatres in London. His melodrama *The Ticket-of-Leave Man* (introducing the detective Hawkshaw) was a great success (it was later filmed in Hollywood, with Tod Slaughter). *Our American Cousin* (1858), which created the character of the brainless and bewhiskered Lord Dundreary, has become notorious as the play Abraham Lincoln was watching when he was assassinated.

William Thackeray (1811–1863)

Thackeray became friendly with John Bowes (the builder of the Bowes Museum) in Paris, where the illegitimate son of the Earl of Strathmore financed the publication of Thackeray's *Flore et Zephyr* in 1836. Thackeray later stayed with his benefactor at Streatlam Castle, near Barnard Castle, between 26 June and 13 July 1841, and assisted in the extremely lively and successful campaign to elect Bowes to represent South Durham in parliament. His host in turn regaled him with the astonishing tragi-comic story of Mary Bowes. Thackeray based his first real novel, the entertaining *Barry Lyndon*, partly upon these scandalous events.

George Macaulay Trevelyan (1876–1962)

Trevelyan was the son of George Otto Trevelyan and like him, belongs to the great tradition of historians in the North East. His works include remarkable books on Garibaldi, for which he walked every mile of the great man's campaigns. His nostalgic *English Social History* (1944) was a best-seller. Trevelyan's view of literature was that it should not be a set of intellectual conundrums: 'It is joy, joy in our inmost heart.'

His love of walking and Northumberland are declared in his essay on the Middle Marches of Northumberland, published in the *Independent Review* in 1904:

In Northumberland alone both heaven and earth are seen: we walk all day on long ridges, high enough to give far views of moor and valley, and the sense of solitude above the world below . . . It is the land of far horizons, where the piled or drifted shapes of gathered vapour are for ever moving along the farthest ridge of hills, like the procession of long primaeval ages that is written in tribal mounds and Roman camps and Border towers on the breast of Northumberland.

George Otto Trevelyan (1838–1928)

A nephew of Lord Macaulay, Trevelyan lived at Wallington Hall for over forty years. He was elected as Liberal M.P. for Tynemouth in 1865 and held several important political offices. However, he also wrote a number of works set in India, including *Cawnpore* (1865): *The Ladies in Parliament* (1869) contains his humorous writings. *Interludes in Prose and Verse* appeared in 1905.

In later life he wrote notable works of biography and history, including *The Life and Letters of Lord Macaulay* (1876).

Jane Turner (fl. 1653)

Jane Turner's autobiographical *Choice Experiences* (1653), written at a time of religious upheaval in England, tells of her Presbyterian childhood in Newcastle, Berwick and London, her conversion to the Baptists, her brief spell with the Quakers and her decision to leave them and return to the Baptist fold.

In 1654, the Quaker preacher Thomas Burrough, though he himself had once had doubts, wrote very unsympathetically of Jane, who had questioned the existence of God in her despair. It is noteworthy that although she can be regarded as conservative in her religious views, Jane presents her religious experience as quite separate from that of her husband.

Of the radical religious groups of the time, the Quakers started almost exclusively in the north, where Burrough travelled a good deal. He takes pride in this in terms which express some of the thought behind the present compilation:

O thou North of England, who art counted as desolate and barren, and reckoned the least of the nations, yet out of thee did the branch spring and the star rise which gives light unto all the region round about.

This was written in 1655 and taken from Burrough's works, published (1672) in the sonorous prose of the time as: *The Memorable Works of a Son of Thunder and Consolation.*

William Turner (1508–1568)

Turner was born in Morpeth and educated at Pembroke Hall, Cambridge, where he became a firm Puritan. In 1538, he published his *Libellus de re herbaria*, which was the first book to give localities for native British plants. As a result of his uncompromising religious beliefs, Turner suffered several spells of exile abroad but used his time well to increase his scientific knowledge, particularly in Italy, where he took his medical doctorate. He returned to England in

1547, and a year later wrote *The Names of Herbes in Greke, Latine, Englishe, Duche and Frenche* in which he announced his intention of producing a Latin herbal. He changed his mind, however, and used English when writing the first part of his *New Herball* in 1551, the year he was appointed Dean of Wells. Ultimately running to three volumes, the book was a landmark in the history of both botany and herbalism, because it gave physicians their first chance to read in their own language an original study of the plants which were so important to their profession. Turner's decision to write in English also assisted in promoting the language as a medium for the communication of philosophical and scientific ideas.

Turner's work broke new ground in the thoroughness and accuracy of its scientific observation. During his lifetime, he was credited with the first sighting and identification of more than 300 native species of plants and is said to have introduced lucerne into this country.

Turner also produced works on ornithology, ichthyology and mineralogy, together with a great many religious tracts. Compelled to leave his post as Dean of Wells when the Catholic Mary Tudor became queen, he regained it in 1558.

Turner's racy and vivid style is that of a vigorous scholar, as much at home in the pastures as in the pulpit. He intersperses his charming plant descriptions with acerbic social comment and ridicule of the fanciful notions which over time had become established in plant lore. Turner was given the title 'Father of English Botany' as long ago as 1790. In 1989, the Mid-Northumberland Arts group (MidNAG), in association with Carcanet, published the first edition of Turner's book in 400 years.

John Udall (1560–1592)

Udall was a puritan divine who contended against the bishops in his three volumes of sermons, as well as in powerful anonymous pamphlets. After being dismissed from his living in Kingston on Thames in July 1588, he was invited to preach in Newcastle. He did so for a year from December 1588, becoming as Charleton puts it, 'a shining light in Newcastle'.

He was summoned to London in December 1589, in connection with the celebrated *Martin Marprelate* tracts against the bishops. How much Udall had helped his friend John Penry in this affair remains obscure; Penry had passed through Newcastle some three months previously, but had merely saluted Udall at his door, according to the latter. At all events, Udall was arrested for the earlier writings he now acknowledged. Condemned to death, he refused to recant; pardoned in June 1592, he died soon after. His Hebrew grammar and dictionary, entitled *The Key to the Holy Tongue*, was published in 1593.

Sir John Vanbrugh (1664–1726)

In this age of specialisation, Vanbrugh's double achievement as playwright and architect seems remarkable indeed. His first play, *The Relapse*, written in 1696, was a great triumph, the character of Lord Foppington being especially memorable. It was followed shortly afterwards by another success, *The Provoked Wife*. Both have retained their popularity with modern theatre-goers.

Vanbrugh was apparently entirely untrained as an architect when the Earl of Carlisle invited him to design a new house at Castle Howard near York in 1699. Jonathan Swift summed up the general surprise: 'Van's genius, without thought or lecture/ is hugely turned to architecture.' Castle Howard became familiar to many when it was used for the television version of Evelyn Waugh's *Brideshead Revisited*. However, this dramatic baroque style of Vanbrugh and Hawksmoor was a short-lived phenomenon. The sedate Georgian architecture of southern England was soon to prevail, and after Vanbrugh's death, the general opinion on the architect of Blenheim Palace was wittily expressed by Abel Evans:

> Lie heavy on him, Earth! for he
> Laid many heavy loads on thee!

The Vanbrughian style was, however, peculiarly suited to the north, which Vanbrugh preferred to the 'tame and sneaking south'. In Berwick upon Tweed, whose magnificently intact Elizabethan ramparts of 1558 testify to its status as a vulnerable frontier town, the attractive barracks, begun in 1717, are the earliest in Britain (before that, troops were quartered on the local people). Vanbrughian in style, they are now known to be by Hawksmoor. Vanbrugh certainly designed the Morpeth Town Hall, though the fire of 1869 reduced its effect considerably. He also worked in County Durham at Lumley Castle. It was at Seaton Delaval, however, that Vanbrugh fully realised his dramatic vision. It was his last (1718–28) and, in the opinion of many, his greatest house. Built for Admiral Delaval, who was not disposed to 'starve the design', it stands massively compact and powerful. As Sir Nikolaus Pevsner remarks: 'No one can forget Seaton Delaval.'

Jules Verne (1828–1905)
In 1859, Jules Verne, while travelling to London from Scotland, passed through the North East by train, and was struck by the multitude of chimneys and nocturnal fires in the coalfield – 'a terrifying nightscape'. In this, his first full-length written narrative (translated as *Backwards to Britain*), he was greatly taken by the fact that some mines ran out under the sea-bed. Captain Nemo's crew in *Twenty Thousand Leagues under the Sea* obtain coal from subterranean seams 'like the mines of Newcastle'.

Brian Walton (c 1599–1661)
Though some accounts have Walton's birthplace as Seamer in Cleveland, it seems more likely that he was born in Northumberland, and attended Queen Elizabeth's Grammar School in Newcastle. He was probably the son of Brian Walton, who was apprenticed to William Marley, a Newcastle merchant, in 1591.

Walton's career in the church had many changes of fortune, but he was eventually appointed Bishop of Chester in 1660. His great claim to fame is his *London Polyglott Bible*, in nine languages, published in six volumes between 1653 and 1657. Though he was assisted by several other scholars, Walton's was the driving force behind the project. Walton's other works include *An Introduction to Oriental Languages* (1654) and *Considerator Considered* (1659), a defence of the Polyglott.

Beatrice Webb (1858–1943)

The celebrated Beatrice Potter (later Beatrice Webb), stayed at the Bath Hotel in Tynemouth (now the Royal Sovereign Hotel, Bath Terrace), from early September to 16 October 1891, after spending a busy week at the Trades Union Congress in Newcastle. Sidney Webb joined her later in Tynemouth for two weeks, discreetly staying at another hotel while pretending to be her secretary. This was 'a blessed time,' says Beatrice, as the two toiled away at her book on trade unionism, with brief intervals of 'human nature' over cigarettes and afternoon tea.

Drudgery in offices and trudging to interviews took up much time; one of her meetings seems to have been with Sir Hugh Bell, Gertrude Bell's father. Beatrice sent Sidney to interview the 'Good Intent Coopers' the evening before his departure, and both spent the day before that in a Newcastle pub, interviewing plumbers. Such was the dedication of the Webbs, who helped to lay the foundations of the welfare state. Founders of the London School of Economics in 1895, they were prominent figures in the labour movement throughout their long lives, consorting with such glamorous figures as Shaw and Wells. They appear in the latter's novel *The New Machiavelli* as rather over-dedicated folk (Beatrice Webb had 'pro bono publico' inscribed in her wedding ring).

Interestingly, the director of the London School of Economics from 1919–1937 was William Beveridge, whose name is associated with the great Beveridge Report of 1943 and associated welfare state legislation. He and his wife are buried in the churchyard at Thockrington in Northumberland, near to Carrycoats Hall, which he regarded as a second home.

The Webbs produced many books together, and Beatrice wrote two volumes of autobiography, *My Apprenticeship* (1926) and *Our Partnership* (1948); her absorbing diary is also a classic of its kind. Oddly, though she had read Harriet Martineau's autobiography, she does not refer to the latter's long residence in Tynemouth in her diary entry for this period.

Cookson Street, off Westgate Road in Newcastle, is the site of the old St Philip's vicarage, described by Beatrice Webb as 'badly built and designed, but pleasantly appointed'. For five weeks in the summer of 1900, the Webbs stayed there with the vicar, William Moll, a member of the Fabian Society, while they studied the workings of Newcastle local government (they were not impressed). The house was well furnished with theological books and the Webbs took some with them on their holiday break to Bamburgh. Beatrice Webb tells us that 'a remarkable Newcastle man, Dr Merz,' gave them his own *History of Thought* to read. On the coast at Bamburgh, they spent three weeks 'lying in a tent on the sand, watching the sea, or cycling over moorland and mountain, or wading out to rocks or islands – a quite enchanting holiday'.

John Wesley (1703–1791)

The founder of Methodism had been taken aback at the prevalence of drunkenness and swearing 'even from the mouths of little children' when he came to Newcastle, but he soon developed a fondness for the town and its people. He preached at the Sandgate on 30

March 1742, as he records in his journal: 'I never saw so large a number of people together, either in Moorfields or at Kennington . . . After preaching, the poor people were ready to tread me under foot out of pure love and kindness.'

Wesley made Newcastle the northern headquarters of his Methodist movement. The Orphan House in Northumberland Street (now marked by a plaque) was where Wesley was living in 1745, when Newcastle was fortified with some two hundred guns against the advancing Bonny Prince Charlie. The Orphan House was outside the walls, but Wesley was undaunted: 'Nay, but the Lord is a wall of fire to all that trust in Him . . .' He also noted that the cannon on Newgate and Pilgrim Street Gate would be a sure protection!

It was at the Orphan House that Wesley met Grace Murray, the widow of a Geordie seafarer. Grace nursed him when he was ill there in 1746, and Wesley thought he had found his helpmate at last. However, his relations with women were constantly bedevilled by misunderstanding, and Grace eventually wed another. Wesley thereupon impulsively married the widow of a London merchant, who tormented him for 30 years. She was even seen to haul the diminutive Wesley across the room by his hair.

In 1778 we find Doctor Johnson and Boswell discussing Wesley's encounter with a Newcastle girl who had seen a ghost. Johnson was inclined to dismiss the story, but Boswell asked him to write a letter of introduction to the preacher. Boswell presented it to Wesley in Edinburgh, but reports: 'His state of the evidence as to the ghost did not satisfy me.'

Wesley's fantastic energy enabled him to preach 40,000 sermons in his lifetime and his literary output was also considerable. His *Journal* in particular is a pleasure to read and contains many interesting references to the North East in particular. He and his brother Charles seem to have visited Morpeth, Alnwick and Berwick on no fewer than 24 occasions. It was in Newcastle that he wrote the Rules of his church, which were also first printed here in 1743 by John Gooding in the Side. For those inclined to complain about the local weather, Wesley's remark of 1759, the words of a man who had travelled many thousands of miles around the country, should give food for thought!

> Certainly if I did not believe there was another world, I would spend all my summers here, as I know no place in Great Britain comparable to it for pleasantness.

Beyond Broad Chare and Love Lane, where Milk Market turns sharply left uphill towards the Keelmens Hospital, stands a granite obelisk commemorating Wesley's death in 1791.

Robert Westall (1929–1993)

Robert Westall was one of the most original and striking of modern writers for children; his book *The Machine-Gunners* would be on any teacher's list of classroom readers.

Westall was born at 7 Vicarage Street, North Shields and the family moved to 18 Balkwell Green when Robert was about five years old. He attended Tynemouth Municipal High School before going on to study fine art at King's College, Newcastle and the Slade

School in London. He later held a number of teaching posts and eventually became an antique dealer in Cheshire.

The Machine-Gunners (1975) was his first book and it won him the prestigious Carnegie Medal. Set in Tynemouth (Garmouth) during the war, it concerns the theft by boys of a machine-gun from a crashed German bomber. Described as wonderfully vivid and forceful, it has been televised by the BBC, as has *The Watch House*, a ghost story linked with the famous Tynemouth institution. *Fathom Five* is set in the Haven, the Fish Quay and Low Street, North Shields, whose demolition Westall deeply regretted, pointing out that in Whitby and Scarborough such streets are treasured.

Though Westall is a realistic writer, concerned with human relationships, he does use the supernatural at times to sharpen his portrayal. *The Wind Eye* actually has Saint Cuthbert affecting a family of today.

Westall kept an exile's love for his home town and was pleased at the restoration of the Watch House and those Georgian gems – the High and Low Lights. The clear river (grebes fishing off Tynemouth pier) and the absence of shipping were a great contrast with his youth when ships were moored three deep in the Tyne and the water was so dirty only black-jack could survive in it. He would have loved to see the river full of pleasure craft but was worried about vandalism and what he called 'the blind following after southern values.'

North Tyneside Council have now established a Robert Westall trail, featuring locations described in the novelist's work. A plaque has been erected in Vicarage Street.

John Mackay Wilson (1804–35)

Wilson was born in Tweedmouth. After some years of lecturing and writing plays and poetry, he became editor of the *Berwick Advertiser* in 1832. By then, however, he had become addicted to the bottle.

The six volumes of his *Tales of the Border* (1834–40) had originally appeared in weekly parts, and after Wilson's death they were continued for his widow with Alexander Leighton as editor. A new edition by Leighton extended to twenty volumes, (1857–59), and his 1869 revision added four more volumes.

Ludwig Wittgenstein (1889–1951)

One of the most influential and charismatic of twentieth century British thinkers, Wittgenstein was professor of philosophy at Cambridge between 1939 and 1947. His famous *Tractatus* (1922), the only book he published in his lifetime, had set limits on what language could legitimately do, and stated that a good deal of conventional discourse was literally meaningless.

During the war, Wittgenstein worked as a porter at Guy's Hospital in London, where there is a plaque, and also at the Royal Victoria Infirmary in Newcastle, where he is not commemorated. (The late broadcaster Brian Redhead once remarked on Radio 4 that he had been wheeled into the operating theatre at the RVI by Wittgenstein.) He worked at the RVI for almost a year in 1943–44, living for some time at Mrs Moffat's house, 28 Brandling Park, on the other side of the Great North Road.

He was absorbed in his work with a team studying wounds (he is said to have used himself as a guinea-pig) and, according to Ray Monk's fine biography, was uncommunicative and went to the 'flicks' every night – though he could never remember anything he saw. Conceivably, as he was extremely fond of strident musicals starring Betty Hutton and Carmen Miranda, he was shy of admitting his choice of film. Whether this was a help or a distraction from serious thinking is unclear. At all events, when a visiting lecturer gave a paper at the university, Wittgenstein ended up taking over the ensuing discussion. Always an intense individual (he brandished a poker at Karl Popper at a Cambridge meeting in 1946) his colleagues feared his talking shop and refused to take him on their relaxing walks along the Roman Wall, though he did visit Durham.

Wittgenstein's ideas on language had been changing since the 1930s and his *Philosophical Investigations*, published posthumously in 1953, point to the variety and open-endedness of everyday language, thus rejecting the perfect logical model of the *Tractatus*, proposing language as a tool-kit, rather than a calculus, as it has been aptly put.

Dorothy Wordsworth (1771–1855)

After her mother's death, Dorothy had lived for ten years in Halifax with her relative Miss Threlkeld, before coming to Newcastle in December 1794. There she resided with the cousins of Miss Threlkeld, in Northumberland Place. In January 1795, she wrote:

> I have been at Newcastle more than a month and am very happy in the company of our good friends the Miss Griffiths who are very chearful pleasant companions, and excellent women.

Her brother William was also in Northumberland Place around 31 January 1795. Dorothy Wordsworth left Newcastle in March or April, and spent at least three weeks at Sockburn Farm near Darlington, where she renewed her friendship with Mary Hutchinson. After William's marriage to Mary, Dorothy remained a part of the household. Her celebrated journals, as well as being an invaluable record of the poet's life and work, are notable for the poetic quality of her descriptive prose; they also served as inspiration for Wordsworth's own poetry.

William Wordsworth (1770–1850)

Apart from the Newcastle visit in 1795, the most celebrated of the Romantic poets has more associations with the North East of England than is commonly realised. After their trip to Germany in 1799, William and Dorothy Wordsworth, together with Coleridge, made the farm at Sockburn their base for most of the year. Wordsworth did a great deal of work, and Coleridge began his tormenting affair with Sara Hutchinson. Though the Wordsworths settled in Grasmere and Rydal for the rest of their lives, there were visits to the Hutchinson homes at Bishop Middleham in Durham, and at Scarborough, until Wordsworth married Mary Hutchinson in 1802.

In 1838 Wordsworth accompanied Miss Fenwick into Northumberland, apparently to visit Holy Island and perhaps Miss Fenwick's old home at Edlingham on the way. After that, they would go to Durham and separate, Wordsworth proceeding to Henry Taylor's house in Witton-le-Wear. The return trip was to be via Teesdale and Alston Moor.

When Wordsworth arrived in Newcastle, he was shown round the city by John Hernaman, editor of the *Newcastle Journal*, founded in 1832. Wordsworth then went off to Tynemouth and North Shields, apparently to see some cousins. The *Newcastle Journal* for 7 July, 1838 mentions his trip to Tynemouth, 'after inspecting the magnificent buildings which adorn our town'.

Wordsworth went on to Warkworth and was later to recall 'bleak Northumbria's coast' and its 'screaming Sea-mews' in his poem about Grace Darling, written in 1842. At Durham, Wordsworth received a D.C.L. It was Durham's first such award but Wordsworth was disappointed that the ceremony was not in Latin.

The Darlington museum owns a pair of Wordsworth's socks, finely knitted (and darned), and with a WW tag sewn on. The provenance of the socks is uncertain, but they may indeed have come from Sockburn.

John Wycliffe (c 1329–1384)

'The Morning Star of the Reformation', the most significant English churchman of his time, was born in or close to Wycliffe-on-Tees, a member of the ancient family celebrated by Sir Walter Scott in *Rokeby*, where Oswald and Wilfrid Wycliffe are characters. Wycliffe went to Balliol College at Oxford, which had been founded by the Balliols of nearby Barnard Castle and became a celebrated lecturer in theology and philosophy. He was Master of Balliol at 36.

In his religious writings, mainly in Latin, but latterly in English, Wycliffe came to attack Rome's control of the English church, denying the validity of confession, indulgences and eventually, transubstantiation. He asserted the right of every man to examine the bible for himself and instituted a project for translating the bible into the vernacular, though this was officially prohibited. The idea, propounded in *De Civile Dominio* (1376) that all authority, whether of church or state, was founded in grace, and that the wicked forfeited their right to rule, had major political implications. Contemporaries sought to establish a connection between his teaching and the Peasant's Revolt of 1381, though Wycliffe condemned the rising.

In 1382 Wycliffe was finally condemned for heresy after several attempts had been made, though for some reason he was not judged and was left to live out his days in peace. In 1428, however, his bones were dug up, burned and thrown into the River Swift.

Wycliffe's ideas, spread by his 'poor priests', gained a wide following in England, where his adherents were known as 'Lollards' (from the Flemish word for 'mumblers'). A strong supporter of Wycliffe's ideas was Sir John Oldcastle, the distant model for Shakespeare's Falstaff. Though the Lollards were brutally suppressed (and Oldcastle 'hanged and burnt hanging'), their influence persisted down to the Protestant Reformation. The importance of Wycliffe's translation project, marking as it does the beginning of a biblical tradition in English prose, can hardly be exaggerated. His ideas are also reflected in the poetry of Chaucer and Langland's *Piers Plowman* (c 1367–70).

The North East can also take pride, at one remove, in the work of William Tyndale (1484?–1536). The Tyndales had moved south to Gloucestershire from Langley Castle during the Wars of the Roses, possibly in the 1460s. They also changed their tell-tale name to Hutchins, the name Tyndale bore at Oxford. Tyndale's great translation of the bible into English was the foundation of all future such undertakings.

Arthur Young (1741–1820)

Young was the great propagandist of the Agricultural Revolution, best known for his *Tour of Ireland* (1780) and, particularly, *Travels in France* (1792). However, he also wrote *A Six Months Tour through the North of England* in 1771.

By contrast with Defoe, say, or Smollett, we find a tone of Romantic delight in his fine descriptions of the Tees, before he travelled on to Durham through fields yellow with mustard flowers. The form in which table mustard is now sold in the United Kingdom dates from 1720, about which time Mrs Clements of Durham hit on the idea of grinding the seed in a mill and sifting the flour from the husk. The bright yellow farina thus produced under the name of 'Durham Mustard' pleased the taste of George I and rapidly attained wide popularity.

After marvelling at Durham Castle and Cathedral, Young and his pregnant wife set off across the moors on horseback to High Force:

> The whole river (no trifling one) divided by one rock, into two vast torrents pours down a perpendicular precipice of near forscore feet: The deluging force of the water throws up such a foam and misty rain, that the sun never shines without a large and brilliant rain-bow appearing . . .

Young describes the wooden coal waggon roads near Newcastle, and sees Crawley's ironworks – 'supposed to be the greatest manufactory of the kind in Europe'.

In Northumberland, Young admired the Wallington Hall estate, then owned by the Blacketts. The roads were excellent, and Young was struck by the fine fencing and hedging. At Alnwick he was pleased with Robert Adam's work on prettifying the castle in the gothick style.

Like any agriculturist, particularly of his period, he deplored waste ground and found 600,000 acres of it in Northumberland, almost half the county: he was, however, impressed by a carrot-grower at Hetton. Young and his wife reached Berwick before turning back towards Carlisle (taking in a walk along the Roman Wall on the way).

Yevgeni Zamyatin (1884–1937)

> Often in the evening as I was returning from the yard in my little Renault, I would be met with a dark, blinded city, all lights extinguished. This meant that German Zeppelins were about and their bombs would soon be crashing down. At night, sitting at home, I would listen to the explosions, some far away, some near at hand, as I checked through [icebreaker] drawings and worked on my novel about the English – *Islanders*.

So writes Zamyatin, who had been sent to England in 1916 by the Russian government to oversee the construction of a number of ice-breakers at Armstrong Whitworth in Low Walker, and Swan Hunter in Wallsend. He also visited South Shields and Sunderland. These vessels included the *Sviatogor*, later re-named *Krasin*, which became the most famous ship in the world in 1928 for its role in rescuing Nobile's Arctic airship expedition. This story was filmed as *The Red Tent* with Peter Finch and Sean Connery.

Zamyatin, unusually for a marine engineer, was also a promising writer, and the culture-shock of arriving among the well-to-do of Jesmond, where he lived at 19 Sanderson Road, stung him into producing two novellas, *Islanders* and *A Fisher of Men*, which made savage fun of them in brilliant style. Zamyatin was exasperated by the way the Jesmondians always repressed spontaneity in favour of order. Later on, however, it seems that Zamyatin became rather Jesmondian himself. Back in Russia – where he was a major figure in the literary world before emigrating to Paris in 1931 – he was known as 'the Englishman', wore tweeds and smoked a pipe.

Harold Heslop was struck by this, when the two met in Leningrad in 1930, even though he did not know of Zamyatin's residence on Tyneside. Zamyatin picked up Heslop's accent at once and told him he liked the Geordies and particularly their musical dialect, though he could never manage it himself. He did come out with 'Sooth Sheels' though.

In *Islanders* the citizens of Jesmond are dominated by the repellent Reverend Dewley, vicar of St Enoch's (actually St George's, Jesmond). Happiness by time-table is his creed. Even Mrs Dewley's needs are catered for every third Saturday.

A Fisher of Men is set in London, but is stuffed with Newcastle allusions. The extensive boating lake and island, where respectable banker Mr Craggs, torch in hand, goes in search of hanky-panky after dark – and supplements his income with a little blackmail – is clearly Leazes Park lake in Central Newcastle.

This all finds nightmarish reflection in *We*, written only a year or so after Zamyatin's return to Russia. In this, the first of the great modern anti-utopias, we find Vicar Dewley's dreams have come true; every hour in the One State is accounted for in the Table of Hourly Commandments. Privacy is non-existent and the city is walled off from the free, dirty, natural and disordered world outside. The uniformed 'numbers' (no one has names) are not unhappy, but it is a rational happiness imposed from above, leaving no room for human freedom and variety. Life in the One State is characterised by regimented obedience to the Benefactor and his Guardians.

It is clear that Zamyatin's Newcastle experience prompted him to imagine such a state, and there are many hidden references in *We* to Newcastle and the working practices in the Tyne shipyards. Even the numbers of the main characters belong to the specification of Zamyatin's favourite icebreaker!

We was banned in the USSR until 1988 (when it came out alongside *Nineteen Eighty-Four* neatly enough): in this country it has long been a Penguin Modern Classic. Orwell read it in French and considered that Huxley's *Brave New World* must have been influenced by

95

it: however, it is Orwell's book which seems to have the more striking parallels with Zamyatin's work. Can we not say that Tyneside, albeit at one remove, produced one of the most influential novels of the latter half of the century?

Index

(The numbers refer to pages. Individual references over many pages are sometimes aggregated, eg 20–41.)